GW01158931

The Musician's Tech Toolbox-Essential Technical Tips and Equipment Know-How for Musicians

Neil J Milliner

Published by Neil J Milliner, 2024.

While every precaution has been taken in the preparation of this book, the publisher assumes no responsibility for errors or omissions, or for damages resulting from the use of the information contained herein.

THE MUSICIAN'S TECH TOOLBOX-ESSENTIAL TECHNICAL TIPS AND EQUIPMENT KNOW-HOW FOR MUSICIANS

First edition. October 20, 2024.

Copyright © 2024 Neil J Milliner.

ISBN: 979-8224869602

Written by Neil J Milliner.

Also by Neil J Milliner

Artful Investments: Enhancing Your Property Value Through Fine Art
E-commerce SEO Strategies: Selling Online Successfully
Fast Track Your Songwriting Career-Essential Tips and Hints to
Master Your Craft and Build a Lasting Career
The Ultimate Singer's Guide-Practical Tips to Improve Your Voice and
Achieve Your Vocal Dreams
Branding & Networking Success for Bands
Mastering Fan Engagement-Pro-Level Hints to Create Authentic
Connections and Build Loyalty
Mastering Live Performance & Touring-Pro Level Tips and Hints to
Elevate Your Stage Presence and Tour Like a Pro
Music Production Mastery-Step-by-Step Tutorials to Fast-Track Your
Way to Professional Success
The Musician's Tech Toolbox-Essential Technical Tips and Equipment
Know-How for Musicians
The Ultimate Musician's Website Guide-Step-by-Step Tutorials to
Engage Fans and Showcase Your Talent

Contents

1

2

Quick Guide to Mastering Vocal EQ and Compression in 10 Minutes for Professional Sound

Achieving a professional-sounding vocal track is one of the key steps in music production. Two essential tools that can dramatically enhance your vocals are EQ and compression. While these tools may seem complicated, you can quickly master the basics to make your vocal recordings sound clear, polished, and well-balanced.

This quick guide walks you through the essentials of vocal EQ and compression in 10 minutes, helping you shape your voice like a pro.

Step 1: Understanding Vocal EQ

EQ (EQUALIZATION) IS a tool used to adjust specific frequencies in your vocal recordings. With proper EQ, you can remove unwanted tones, enhance clarity, and bring out the best parts of your voice.

Key EQ Zones for Vocals:

- Low-End (20–100 Hz): Often contains unwanted rumble or low-frequency noise. Use a high-pass filter to remove everything below 80 Hz.

- Low Mids (100–300 Hz): Adds warmth but can also create muddiness. Cut slightly around 200 Hz if your vocals sound too thick.

- Midrange (300–1,000 Hz): Controls vocal clarity. Boost around 400–600 Hz to add definition or reduce this zone if your voice sounds boxy.

- High Mids (1,000–5,000 Hz): Adds presence and intelligibility. Boost around 2,000–4,000 Hz to make your voice cut through the mix.

- High-End (5,000–10,000 Hz): Adds brightness and clarity. A gentle boost in this range brings a polished shine to your vocals.

- Air (10,000 Hz and above): Adds airiness and openness. Boost sparingly to add sparkle without introducing harshness.

How to EQ Quickly:

- Use a High-Pass Filter: Start by cutting out any frequencies below 80 Hz to clean up low-end rumble.

- Tame Muddiness: If your voice sounds too boomy, reduce the 200 Hz range slightly to add clarity.

- Add Presence: Boost the 3,000 Hz range to make your vocals stand out without being harsh.

- Enhance Air: For a professional shine, gently boost around 10,000 Hz.

Step 2: Understanding Compression

COMPRESSION SMOOTHS out the dynamic range of your vocals by controlling the loud and quiet parts, making your vocal track sound consistent and balanced. This helps your voice sit comfortably in the mix without sudden volume spikes.

Key Compression Terms:

- Threshold: The level at which compression kicks in. Set this to the point where the vocal volume starts to get too loud.

- Ratio: Controls how much compression is applied. A ratio of 3:1 or 4:1 is ideal for vocals—strong but not too aggressive.

- Attack: How quickly the compressor responds. A slower attack (around 10–20 ms) lets through the vocal transients, keeping your vocals punchy.

- Release: How quickly the compression fades. A medium release (around 50–100 ms) ensures smooth control without squashing your vocals.

- Makeup Gain: After compression, your overall volume might be lower. Use makeup gain to bring the vocal volume back to its original level.

How to Compress Quickly:

- Set the Threshold: Lower the threshold until you see 3–5 dB of gain reduction when the vocals hit their loudest points.

- Choose the Right Ratio: Start with a ratio of 3:1 to 4:1. This balances dynamic control without making the vocals sound too flat.

- Adjust Attack and Release: A slow attack around 10 ms allows the natural vocal transients to come through, while a medium release of around 50 ms ensures the vocals stay smooth.

- Apply Makeup Gain: Use makeup gain to compensate for any volume loss caused by compression, ensuring the vocals stay prominent in the mix.

Step 3: Combining EQ and Compression for Professional Sound

ONCE YOU'VE DIALED in your EQ and compression settings, your vocals should sound polished, clear, and well-balanced. Combining both tools ensures that your vocals are both tonally balanced (EQ) and dynamically controlled (compression).

Quick Tips:

- EQ before Compression: It's generally better to use EQ before compression to shape the tonal quality of your vocals, then use compression to control dynamics.

- Listen in Context: Always check your EQ and compression settings while listening to the entire mix, not just the soloed vocals. This ensures your voice sits perfectly with the other instruments.

- Subtle Adjustments: Less is often more. Avoid extreme EQ boosts or heavy compression to keep your vocals sounding natural.

Final Thoughts

MASTERING VOCAL EQ and compression doesn't have to take hours of tweaking. By focusing on key frequency zones and using

compression to control dynamics, you can achieve a professional vocal sound in just 10 minutes. With a little practice, these quick steps will become second nature, and your vocal recordings will always sound clean, polished, and ready for the mix.

Advanced Techniques and Pro Tips for Recording String Instruments with Perfect Clarity

Recording string instruments, whether it's a violin, cello, guitar, or double bass, requires a delicate balance of technique and the right equipment to capture the rich, nuanced sound they produce. Getting a professional, clear recording of string instruments can be challenging, but with the right approach, you can achieve impressive results. Here are some advanced techniques and pro tips to help you record string instruments with perfect clarity.

1. Choose the Right Microphone

THE TYPE OF MICROPHONE you choose plays a critical role in the clarity of your string recordings. While condenser microphones are commonly used for recording strings due to their sensitivity and broad frequency range, ribbon microphones can also be excellent for capturing the natural warmth of the instrument.

- Condenser Microphones: Ideal for capturing detailed and bright sound. The Neumann U87 and Audio-Technica AT4053b are excellent choices.

- Ribbon Microphones: Known for capturing smooth, natural tones, making them ideal for string instruments. Consider using the Royer R-121 for a warm, vintage sound.

Pro Tip: For solo string recordings, consider using a small-diaphragm condenser microphone, as it captures high frequencies with more precision. For a fuller, more ambient sound, a large-diaphragm condenser microphone can be beneficial.

2. Mic Placement: Experiment for Optimal Sound

CORRECT MIC PLACEMENT is essential for getting a clean and clear string recording. The sound of the instrument can change dramatically depending on where you place the mic, and the best positioning will vary depending on the instrument and the room acoustics.

- Close Miking: Placing the microphone close to the instrument (6-12 inches away) will capture a more detailed, direct sound, but be mindful of capturing unwanted sounds like the movement of fingers on strings.

- Room Miking: Placing the microphone further away (around 3 feet) captures more of the instrument's resonance and the room's natural reverb, which can add depth to the recording.

Pro Tip: Use a combination of close mics and room mics for a balanced sound. For example, you could place one mic close to the instrument and a second further away to capture the room's ambience. Blend these tracks during mixing to create a rich, layered sound.

3. Utilize Multiple Microphones for Depth

TO CAPTURE THE FULL tonal range of string instruments, consider using a multi-microphone setup. Different parts of a string instrument resonate in unique ways, and recording from multiple angles can provide a more complete picture of the sound.

- Stereo Miking: Position two microphones in a stereo configuration (like XY or ORTF) to capture a wider sound field and more depth. This technique works particularly well with ensemble recordings.

- Close and Ambient Mic Combo: Place one mic close to the instrument and another at a distance to capture room acoustics. Balance these in post-production for a fuller sound.

Pro Tip: When using multiple microphones, be mindful of phase issues. If the microphones are not positioned carefully, the sound waves might cancel each other out, causing the recording to lose clarity. To avoid this, follow the "3-to-1" rule: make sure each microphone is at least three times the distance apart as it is to the source.

4. Consider the Room Acoustics

STRING INSTRUMENTS are incredibly sensitive to room acoustics, so the space you record in has a significant impact on the clarity and warmth of your recording. Rooms with natural reverb, such as large, open spaces with wooden floors, can enhance the sound of strings. However, in smaller or untreated rooms, excessive reflections can muddy the sound.

- Acoustic Treatment: If your room produces too much reverb or unwanted reflections, consider using bass traps and acoustic panels to control the sound. A well-treated room allows the instrument's natural tone to shine.

- Portable Solutions: If acoustic treatment is not an option, try using gobos or reflection filters around the instrument to minimize reflections and capture a cleaner sound.

Pro Tip: When recording in a room with a lot of reverb, use a close-mic technique to capture more direct sound. Add reverb in post-production if needed, giving you greater control over the final mix.

5. Record at a High Sample Rate

RECORDING AT A HIGHER sample rate (such as 96kHz or 192kHz) can capture more detailed sound, which especially beneficial for string instruments with their complex harmonic content.

This gives you more flexibility in post-production, allowing for more precise editing and higher-quality sound overall.

Pro Tip: If your project allows for it, record at the highest sample rate your equipment can handle. This ensures that every detail of the instrument's sound is captured, which can later be downsampled for final production.

6. Use Proper EQ Techniques

EQ CAN MAKE OR BREAK a string recording. You want to enhance the natural warmth and clarity of the instrument without introducing harshness or muddiness.

- Low-End Control: String instruments, particularly cellos and double basses, can produce low-end rumble that needs to be controlled. Use a high-pass filter to roll off frequencies below 60-80Hz.
- Midrange Boost: Boosting the midrange (500Hz-2kHz) can bring out the character and richness of the instrument.
- High-End Detail: Add a gentle high-frequency boost around 8kHz-10kHz to enhance the brilliance and clarity without making the sound harsh.

Pro Tip: Avoid over-EQing. The goal is to enhance the instrument's natural sound rather than drastically alter it.

7. Compression for Controlled Dynamics

STRING INSTRUMENTS can have wide dynamic ranges, especially in more expressive performances. Compression helps to control these dynamics, ensuring that quieter passages are audible while louder sections don't overpower the mix.

- Light Compression: Use gentle compression (with a ratio of around 2:1 to 4:1) to even out the dynamics while preserving the natural ebb and flow of the performance.

- Attack and Release Settings: Set the attack time long enough to let the transients (the initial sharp sound) through, but short enough to prevent the peaks from being too sharp. Adjust the release time so that the compression returns to normal during quieter sections.

Pro Tip: Use compression sparingly on solo string instruments to maintain their dynamic expression. For ensemble recordings, more compression may be needed to blend the sound smoothly.

8. Post-Production: Reverb and Panning

IN POST-PRODUCTION, you can further enhance your string recordings by using reverb and panning to create a sense of space and depth. Applying reverb can add natural ambiance and make the recording sound more immersive, while panning allows you to position different instruments in the stereo field for a balanced mix.

- Reverb: Use a plate reverb or chamber reverb for a natural, smooth sound that complements the strings. Avoid overloading the mix with too much reverb, as it can make the sound muddy.

- Panning: For ensembles, pan different string instruments across the stereo field to recreate the feeling of a live performance. For solo instruments, keep the sound more centered, with slight panning to give depth.

Pro Tip: Experiment with automation in post-production to adjust reverb and volume levels dynamically, enhancing the emotional impact of the performance.

Conclusion

RECORDING STRING INSTRUMENTS with perfect clarity requires attention to detail, the right equipment, and a few advanced techniques. By choosing the appropriate microphone, mastering mic placement, and refining your post-production processes, you can capture the rich, nuanced sound that makes strings so powerful in music. Keep experimenting and fine-tuning your setup to find what works best for your specific instrument and recording environment. Happy recording!

Step-by-Step Guide to Recording Acoustic Stringed Instruments for Professional Sound Quality

Recording acoustic stringed instruments like guitars, violins, cellos, or mandolins requires special attention to detail to capture their natural, rich tones. Achieving professional sound quality comes from a combination of proper mic placement, environment, and post-production techniques. This guide will walk you through a step-by-step approach to ensure you get the best possible recording.

1. Choose the Right Environment

THE ROOM WHERE YOU record significantly affects the sound quality of your acoustic instrument. An untreated or overly reflective room can add unwanted echoes or muddiness to your recording.

- Tip: If possible, use a room with good natural acoustics, such as a space with soft furnishings, rugs, or even acoustic panels to dampen reflections.

- Alternative: If your recording space is too "live," you can use a small isolation shield or baffle around the instrument to minimize unwanted room sound.

2. Select the Right Microphone

CHOOSING THE APPROPRIATE microphone for your instrument is key. Condenser mics are ideal for capturing the nuanced tones of acoustic instruments, but you can experiment with dynamic mics or ribbon mics depending on the sound you want.

- Large Diaphragm Condenser Mic: Best for recording the body of the instrument, capturing low-end warmth.

- Small Diaphragm Condenser Mic: Excellent for capturing high-end detail and clarity, especially for instruments like violins or mandolins.

- Ribbon Mic: Produces a warm, vintage sound but requires careful placement due to its sensitivity to loud volumes.

3. Optimal Mic Placement

POSITIONING YOUR MICROPHONE(s) properly will make a huge difference in the tone and clarity of your recording. Here are some common techniques:

- For Acoustic Guitar:

- Mic 1 (Body): Place a large diaphragm condenser mic about 6-12 inches from the 12th fret of the guitar neck. This captures a balanced sound without too much boominess from the soundhole.

- Mic 2 (Soundhole): If you're using a second mic, position it 6 inches away from the soundhole to capture more bass frequencies. Be careful, though, as this can introduce muddiness if too close.

- For Violin/Cello:

- Position a small diaphragm condenser mic about 1-2 feet away from the instrument, aimed at where the neck meets the body for a balanced, natural tone.

- Experiment with angling the mic slightly towards the f-holes (on violins, cellos, and other bowed instruments) to capture resonance.

- Tip: Always check for phasing issues when using multiple microphones. Phasing can cause thin, hollow-sounding recordings. Move the mics slightly or use a phase-invert button to correct.

4. Adjust Your Instrument's Positioning

JUST AS IMPORTANT AS mic placement is how the instrument is positioned in relation to the microphone. Different angles will emphasize different tonal characteristics of your instrument.
  - Tip: Have the player experiment with the positioning of their instrument while recording test takes. Sometimes, angling the guitar slightly up or down, or adjusting the distance between the mic and instrument can drastically improve the tone.

5. Control Dynamics During Recording

ACOUSTIC STRINGED INSTRUMENTS can vary in loudness depending on the performance. To prevent clipping or overly quiet passages, make sure to properly adjust the gain on your audio interface or mixing console.
  - Tip: Use a pop filter or windscreen if you're experiencing unwanted noise from a performer's breath or hand movements. Additionally, a compressor can be lightly applied to even out dynamic spikes in the performance without sacrificing the natural expressiveness of the instrument.

6. Record in Multiple Takes

RECORDING IN LAYERS, or takes, allows you to piece together the best parts of each performance for a final, seamless track. Many professional recordings use a composite of multiple takes to create the ideal performance.
  - Tip: Record multiple takes of difficult sections to give yourself options when editing later. For string ensembles, consider recording each part separately for more control during mixing.

7. Post-Production Techniques

ONCE YOU'VE CAPTURED your performance, the magic happens in the mix. Here are a few steps to ensure your recordings sound professional:

- EQ: Begin by cutting low frequencies (under 80Hz) to remove any rumble. Boost around 3-5 kHz to add presence and clarity, but avoid overdoing it, as acoustic instruments should retain their natural warmth.

- Compression: Light compression will help even out dynamics, but avoid squashing the performance. Maintain the instrument's dynamic range for a more organic sound.

- Reverb: Add a touch of natural reverb to give your recording space and depth. A room or plate reverb works well for most acoustic string instruments, but avoid overdoing it—too much reverb can make the instrument sound distant or muddy.

8. Editing and Arrangement

- CLEAN UP UNWANTED Noise: Remove any extraneous sounds like fret noise, finger squeaks, or breaths, unless they enhance the organic feel of the performance.

- Panning: When mixing multiple instruments, consider panning them slightly left or right to create a full, balanced stereo image.

9. Listen Critically

ONCE YOU'VE FINISHED recording and mixing, step away and listen with fresh ears. Reference your recording on different speakers or headphones to ensure it sounds great in a variety of listening environments.

- Tip: Compare your recording to professionally produced tracks of similar instruments to evaluate your sound and adjust accordingly.

Conclusion

RECORDING ACOUSTIC stringed instruments for professional sound quality requires a thoughtful combination of environment, mic placement, and post-production techniques. By following these steps, you'll be able to capture the rich, nuanced tones of your instrument, resulting in a high-quality recording. With the right preparation and attention to detail, you can achieve a polished, professional sound that stands out.

Easy Guide to Converting Audio to MIDI in Any DAW for Music Producers

Converting audio to MIDI is one of the most powerful tools in a music producer's toolkit. It allows you to take a recorded audio performance and turn it into a flexible MIDI sequence that you can manipulate, edit, and experiment with to enhance your production. Whether you want to capture a melody, chord progression, or drum pattern, audio-to-MIDI conversion opens up a world of creative possibilities.

In this easy guide, we'll walk you through how to convert audio to MIDI in different DAWs and share essential tips for getting the most out of this technique.

Why Convert Audio to MIDI?

BEFORE WE DIVE INTO the process, let's briefly touch on why converting audio to MIDI can be a game-changer for producers:

1. Creative Flexibility: You can edit the notes, change the instruments, or apply different virtual synths or sounds to a melody or rhythm you've already recorded.

2. Sound Replacement: Turn a live drum performance into a MIDI sequence, then replace it with samples of your choice for a more polished or electronic sound.

3. Remixing: Audio-to-MIDI conversion makes remixing a track easier because you can extract melodies, chords, and bass lines and rework them.

4. Learning Tool: It's a great way to understand the structure of melodies or chords in a song you admire. By converting it to MIDI, you can study the notes in detail.

Step-by-Step Guide for Converting Audio to MIDI in Popular DAWs

WHILE EACH DAW HAS its own method of converting audio to MIDI, the process is generally straightforward. Here's how you can do it in some of the most commonly used DAWs:

1. Ableton Live

Ableton Live has one of the easiest and most advanced audio-to-MIDI features. It allows you to convert different types of audio with precision, including melodies, harmonies, and drum patterns.

- Step 1: Drag the audio clip you want to convert into Ableton's timeline.

- Step 2: Right-click on the audio clip.

- Step 3: Select one of the following options depending on what you're converting:

- Convert Melody to MIDI (for single-note melodies)

- Convert Harmony to MIDI (for chords or polyphonic sounds)

- Convert Drums to MIDI (for drum or percussive sounds)

- Step 4: Ableton will automatically generate a MIDI track based on the selected conversion.

From here, you can assign the MIDI notes to any virtual instrument, edit the notes, and adjust the performance as you like.

2. Logic Pro

Logic Pro has a built-in function called "Audio to Score" that allows you to convert audio to MIDI. Here's how to do it:

- Step 1: Import your audio file into Logic's timeline.

- Step 2: Double-click on the audio file to open it in the Sample Editor.

- Step 3: Go to the Functions menu and select Convert to MIDI.

- Step 4: Choose the appropriate algorithm based on the type of audio you're converting, such as Monophonic or Polyphonic.

Logic will create a MIDI track with the converted data, allowing you to assign it to any MIDI instrument.

3. FL Studio

FL Studio's Edison tool lets you convert audio to MIDI easily, with some limitations depending on the complexity of the audio.

- Step 1: Import the audio file into Edison.

- Step 2: Right-click the waveform in Edison and select Tools → Convert to Score and Dump to Piano Roll.

- Step 3: FL Studio will convert the audio and generate MIDI in the Piano Roll.

You can now assign the MIDI to any virtual instrument in FL Studio.

4. Studio One

Studio One also supports audio-to-MIDI conversion, especially useful for drums and rhythm patterns.

- Step 1: Import your audio file into Studio One.

- Step 2: Right-click on the audio track and select Detect Transients.

- Step 3: Select the detected transients and right-click again to choose Extract to MIDI.

The MIDI data will now be available on a new track for editing and processing.

5. Cubase

Cubase offers a "VariAudio" feature, ideal for converting monophonic audio into MIDI.

- Step 1: Load your audio file into a track in Cubase.

- Step 2: Select the audio clip, and open the VariAudio panel under the Inspector.

- Step 3: Click Pitch & Warp to analyze the audio file.

- Step 4: Once the notes are detected, right-click and select Extract MIDI.

You can then use the converted MIDI to control any virtual instrument or synth.

Tips for Better Audio-to-MIDI Conversion

1. USE CLEAN AUDIO: For the most accurate conversion, use clean and isolated audio recordings. The less noise and background interference, the more accurate the MIDI will be.

2. Understand Limitations: Audio-to-MIDI conversion works best with monophonic (single-note) lines. Polyphonic or complex sounds may require additional manual tweaking after the conversion.

3. Edit the MIDI Data: The conversion process isn't always perfect. After converting audio to MIDI, check the MIDI notes and make any necessary adjustments in the Piano Roll or MIDI editor.

4. Layering MIDI with Audio: For an interesting effect, you can layer the original audio with the newly converted MIDI for a fuller sound or to create interesting harmonic textures.

5. Experiment with Different Instruments: Once you have your MIDI track, experiment with different virtual instruments, synths, and sounds to find the perfect match for your production.

Conclusion

CONVERTING AUDIO TO MIDI is an essential skill for music producers looking to get more creative control over their recordings. Whether you're working with a melody, chords, or drum patterns, this technique allows you to manipulate and experiment with sounds in ways that aren't possible with raw audio alone. By mastering audio-to-MIDI conversion in your DAW, you open up endless possibilities for remixing, sound design, and creative exploration.

Next time you're working on a track, don't hesitate to try converting audio to MIDI—you might discover new ideas and possibilities that can take your production to the next level!

Step-by-Step Guide to Connecting Studio Monitors to an Audio Interface for Optimal Sound

Setting up your home studio with studio monitors is a game-changer for improving sound accuracy. Unlike regular speakers, studio monitors offer a flat frequency response, giving you a more accurate representation of your recordings. Connecting your studio monitors to an audio interface correctly is essential to achieving the best sound quality and ensuring that your mixes translate well on any playback system.

In this guide, we'll walk you through the step-by-step process of connecting studio monitors to an audio interface, while covering key considerations for optimal sound.

Why Use Studio Monitors with an Audio Interface?

AN AUDIO INTERFACE serves as the bridge between your computer and the monitors, providing high-quality audio output. It ensures that the audio signal from your computer is converted into a format that can be played through your monitors, giving you clear, accurate sound during production.

Studio monitors, when connected properly to your audio interface, provide a true representation of your music without exaggerated bass or treble. This ensures you can make informed decisions during the mixing and mastering process.

Step-by-Step Guide to Connecting Studio Monitors to an Audio Interface

STEP 1: GATHER THE Necessary Equipment

Before connecting your studio monitors to the audio interface, make sure you have the right equipment. Here's what you'll need:
- Studio monitors: A pair of active (powered) monitors.
- Audio interface: Ensure it has balanced outputs.
- Balanced cables: XLR or TRS cables are ideal for optimal sound quality.
- Power source: Both the interface and monitors will need power.

Step 2: Position Your Studio Monitors Correctly

The placement of your studio monitors is crucial for accurate sound. Follow these guidelines for optimal positioning:
- Create an equilateral triangle: Position your monitors and listening position in the shape of an equilateral triangle. The distance between the two monitors should be the same as the distance from each monitor to your ears.
- Height and angle: The tweeters (high-frequency drivers) of your monitors should be at ear level, and the monitors should be angled slightly inward, aiming directly at your listening position.
- Avoid corners: Avoid placing your monitors in the corners of the room, as this can cause an uneven bass response due to sound reflections.

Step 3: Connect the Audio Interface to Your Computer

Before connecting the monitors, start by connecting your audio interface to your computer:
- USB/Thunderbolt: Most audio interfaces use a USB or Thunderbolt connection. Plug the appropriate cable into your interface and connect it to your computer.
- Install drivers: If your interface requires specific drivers, make sure to download and install them from the manufacturer's website to ensure the interface functions properly.

Step 4: Use Balanced Cables for Connecting Monitors to the Interface

Balanced cables, such as XLR or TRS (1/4-inch) cables, are recommended for connecting studio monitors to the audio interface. They reduce noise and interference, ensuring a cleaner sound.

- XLR to XLR: If your audio interface and monitors have XLR inputs and outputs, use an XLR cable for the connection. Plug one end into the balanced output of the interface and the other end into the balanced input of the monitor.

- TRS to TRS: If your monitors have TRS inputs and your interface has TRS outputs, use TRS cables (1/4-inch) to connect the interface to the monitors. TRS cables are also balanced and help prevent signal interference.

> Note: Avoid using unbalanced cables (like RCA or TS), as they are more prone to interference and can result in a noisier signal.

Step 5: Power on Your Monitors and Interface

Once everything is connected, it's time to power on your equipment:

- Power on the audio interface first: Turn on the interface before your studio monitors. This helps prevent any loud pops or noises from damaging your speakers when the system is powered on.

- Power on the monitors: After the interface is on, power up the studio monitors.

Step 6: Adjust Volume Settings

With everything connected and powered up, the next step is to set appropriate volume levels:

- Monitor volume: Start by setting your studio monitors' volume to around 70-80% of their maximum output. This ensures they operate at an optimal level without distortion.

- Interface volume: Use the volume controls on your audio interface to adjust the overall output. Begin at a lower level and gradually increase to find a comfortable listening volume.

- DAW output levels: In your DAW (digital audio workstation), keep the master output level at unity (0 dB). Avoid excessive boosting in the software, as this can lead to clipping or distortion in your mix.

Step 7: Test the Setup

Once your monitors are connected and volumes adjusted, test the setup with an audio track you're familiar with. Listen closely to ensure that:

- The left and right channels are properly balanced.
- There is no hum, hiss, or interference in the signal.
- The monitors are delivering a clear, accurate sound across all frequencies.

Step 8: Optimize the Room's Acoustics

Even with properly connected monitors, your room's acoustics play a major role in how the sound is perceived. Here are a few tips to optimize your room for better sound:

- Acoustic treatment: Add acoustic panels and bass traps to your room to reduce sound reflections and enhance accuracy.
- Monitor isolation pads: Use monitor stands or isolation pads to decouple your monitors from your desk and reduce vibrations that can color the sound.

Common Mistakes to Avoid

- USING UNBALANCED CABLES: Unbalanced cables can introduce noise and interfere with the signal. Always use balanced XLR or TRS cables for the best sound quality.
- Incorrect monitor placement: Poor placement can lead to inaccurate sound. Follow the equilateral triangle method for ideal positioning.
- Volume mismatch: Avoid setting your monitors' volume too high or your interface's output too low. Find a balanced setting for both to ensure optimal performance.

Conclusion

CONNECTING YOUR STUDIO monitors to your audio interface correctly is essential for producing high-quality, professional sound in your home studio. By following this step-by-step guide and using the right equipment, you'll be able to enjoy accurate sound that reflects the true nature of your recordings. Proper positioning, balanced cables, and careful volume adjustments will make all the difference in achieving the best possible audio experience.

With this setup in place, you'll be ready to create and mix music with confidence, knowing that what you hear is an honest representation of your production.

Innovative Soundproofing Methods for a Drum Room: How to Reduce Noise and Improve Acoustics

Drum rooms can be one of the most challenging spaces to soundproof. Drums are loud, and their vibrations can easily travel through walls, floors, and ceilings, making it difficult to contain the noise. Whether you're a professional drummer or a hobbyist, finding effective ways to soundproof your drum room is essential—not only to keep your neighbors happy but also to improve the acoustics of the room for better recordings and practice sessions.

In this blog post, we'll explore some innovative soundproofing methods that can help reduce noise while enhancing the overall acoustic quality of your drum room.

1. Use Mass-Loaded Vinyl (MLV)

MASS-LOADED VINYL (MLV) is a flexible, heavy material that is highly effective at blocking sound. It can be applied to walls, floors, and ceilings to create an additional barrier against noise transmission. MLV works by adding mass to the surfaces of your room, which helps prevent sound waves from passing through.

- Application: MLV can be installed between layers of drywall, under flooring, or even hung as a soundproof curtain around the room.

- Benefits: It's particularly useful for low-frequency sounds like the booming of a bass drum, which are harder to block.

Pro Tip: When using MLV, make sure to seal any gaps or seams to prevent sound leakage.

2. Build a Room-Within-a-Room (Floating Room)

THE CONCEPT OF A ROOM-within-a-room is one of the most effective soundproofing techniques. This involves building a second layer of walls, ceiling, and floor inside your existing drum room, creating an air gap that helps isolate sound.

- How It Works: The air gap between the two layers acts as a sound buffer, preventing vibrations from traveling through the building structure. This method is especially useful for reducing low-frequency sounds that easily travel through solid surfaces.

- Construction: You can use resilient channels, sound isolation clips, and double layers of drywall to create the inner structure, with the outer room acting as a barrier.

Pro Tip: Use dense materials like Green Glue between drywall layers for added soundproofing. Green Glue is a noise-dampening compound that absorbs sound energy.

3. Install Acoustic Panels

WHILE SOUNDPROOFING focuses on blocking sound from escaping, improving the acoustics of your drum room is equally important. Acoustic panels are an excellent solution for reducing echoes and controlling room reflections, which can make your drumming sound clearer and more balanced.

- Types of Acoustic Panels: Choose foam panels, fabric-covered fiberglass panels, or DIY acoustic panels made from sound-absorbing materials.

- Placement: Position acoustic panels strategically on the walls, particularly in areas where sound reflects the most, such as directly behind and in front of the drum kit.

Pro Tip: Combine acoustic panels with bass traps in the corners of the room to absorb low-end frequencies, which can often build up in smaller spaces.

4. Use Drum Shields

DRUM SHIELDS, ALSO known as drum screens or drum cages, are clear acrylic barriers that can be placed around the drum kit to reduce the spread of sound. While they don't completely eliminate noise, drum shields can help control the volume and direction of the sound within the room.

- Benefits: Drum shields are particularly useful in shared studio spaces where drums need to be isolated from other instruments. They also help control the amount of sound that reaches microphones during recordings, leading to cleaner recordings.

- Combined Approach: Drum shields are most effective when used in combination with other soundproofing methods like acoustic panels and soundproof curtains.

Pro Tip: Add sound-absorbing panels around the drum shield to further enhance noise reduction and prevent sound from reflecting back into the room.

5. Install Soundproof Doors and Windows

DOORS AND WINDOWS ARE common weak points in any soundproofing setup. Regular doors and windows allow sound to escape easily, so upgrading to soundproof alternatives is crucial for reducing drum noise.

- Solid-Core Doors: Replace hollow-core doors with solid-core doors, which are much denser and better at blocking sound.

- Soundproof Windows: If possible, install double- or triple-pane windows to block outside noise. For an added layer of soundproofing, use soundproof curtains or acoustic blankets over the windows.

Pro Tip: Use weatherstripping around the door and window frames to seal any gaps where sound might leak out.

6. Soundproof Flooring with Isolation Pads

DRUMS CREATE SIGNIFICANT impact noise, especially through the floor. Using drum risers or isolation pads can help reduce the amount of sound and vibration that travels through the floor and into neighboring rooms.

- Drum Risers: A drum riser lifts the drum kit off the floor and absorbs some of the impact noise. You can build a DIY drum riser using plywood and soundproofing materials like foam and carpet.

- Isolation Pads: Place rubber isolation pads or anti-vibration mats under the drums and cymbal stands to reduce vibrations that would otherwise be transmitted through the floor.

Pro Tip: Combine isolation pads with heavy rugs or carpet underneath the drum kit to further reduce noise.

7. Seal Gaps and Cracks

EVEN THE SMALLEST GAPS in your drum room can allow sound to escape, so it's important to seal any cracks or openings around windows, doors, and walls.

- Acoustic Sealant: Use acoustic caulk or sealant to fill in gaps around doorframes, windowsills, and corners.

- Weatherstripping: Apply weatherstripping around doors and windows to prevent sound leakage. This is a quick and inexpensive way to improve soundproofing without extensive renovations.

Pro Tip: Pay special attention to any electrical outlets, light switches, and ventilation grilles, as these are often overlooked areas where sound can escape.

8. Decoupling with Resilient Channels

DECOUPLING INVOLVES separating two structures to prevent sound from transferring between them. Resilient channels are metal strips installed between drywall and the studs or ceiling joists. These channels create a flexible barrier that prevents sound vibrations from traveling through the walls and ceiling.

- How It Works: Resilient channels effectively "float" the drywall, minimizing contact with the structure of the room and reducing sound transmission.

- Where to Use: Install resilient channels on both walls and ceilings for the best results.

Pro Tip: Use resilient channels in combination with double layers of drywall and Green Glue for maximum soundproofing.

Conclusion

SOUNDPROOFING A DRUM room requires a combination of methods to reduce noise transmission and improve room acoustics.

DIY Guide to Making Acoustic Panels for Professional Sound Treatment in Your Home Studio

Creating a professional-sounding environment in your home studio is essential for producing high-quality recordings and mixes. One of the most effective ways to control sound reflections and reduce unwanted noise is by installing acoustic panels. While commercial panels can be expensive, making your own DIY acoustic panels is both cost-effective and relatively simple. Here's a step-by-step guide on how to craft your own acoustic panels for superior sound treatment in your home studio.

Why Use Acoustic Panels?

BEFORE DIVING INTO the DIY process, it's important to understand why acoustic panels are essential. In untreated rooms, sound waves bounce off walls, ceilings, and floors, causing unwanted reflections, echoes, and reverb. Acoustic panels absorb these reflections, allowing you to hear a more accurate representation of your recordings and mixes.

Materials You'll Need:

1. Wood for the Frame (usually pine or another softwood)

- 1" x 4" planks (for a 2x4 foot panel)

2. Absorption Material

- Owens Corning 703 or Rockwool (mineral wool) insulation is the most effective material for sound absorption. You'll need enough for the size of your panels.

3. Fabric

- Use breathable fabric (like burlap or cotton) to cover your panels. Avoid fabric that's too thick or non-breathable, as it will reflect sound rather than allow it to pass through to the absorption material.

4. Staple Gun and Staples

- To secure the fabric to the wood frame.

5. Wood Screws

- To hold the frame together.

6. Mounting Hardware

- Picture-hanging brackets or French cleats to mount the panels on the wall.

Step 1: Measure and Cut the Wood for the Frame

The standard size for acoustic panels is 2x4 feet, but you can adjust based on the needs of your space. Measure and cut the wood planks into the following dimensions:

- Two pieces of 4 feet for the long sides.
- Two pieces of 2 feet for the short sides.

These pieces will form the rectangular frame for your panel.

Step 2: Build the Frame

Using wood screws, connect the planks to form a sturdy rectangular frame. Ensure that the joints are tight and square. You can reinforce the frame with corner brackets if needed, but it's not always necessary for light-duty use.

Step 3: Insert the Absorption Material

Once your frame is built, place the mineral wool or fiberglass insulation inside the frame. It should fit snugly without gaps. These materials are highly effective at absorbing sound, especially in the mid-to-high frequency range, which makes them ideal for acoustic treatment.

Step 4: Cut and Attach the Fabric

Next, cut your breathable fabric to size. Make sure the fabric is large enough to wrap around the entire panel, covering the front and wrapping around the sides and back of the frame.

Lay the fabric flat on the ground, place the frame with the absorption material face down on the fabric, and begin pulling the fabric tightly around the edges. Using a staple gun, staple the fabric to the back of the wooden frame. Make sure the fabric is smooth and taut to avoid wrinkles, as this will improve the appearance and performance of the panel.

Step 5: Seal the Back

For added durability and aesthetics, you can cover the back of the panel with an additional piece of fabric or a thin plywood board. While not necessary for acoustic performance, this step can make your panels more polished and long-lasting.

Step 6: Mount the Panels

Once the panels are finished, you'll need to mount them on your walls. French cleats or picture-hanging brackets are effective methods for securing the panels to your walls. The positioning of your panels is crucial for optimal sound treatment.

- First reflection points: Place panels at the points on the walls where sound from your speakers first hits, usually at ear level.

- Ceiling: Hanging panels from the ceiling (also known as "clouds") can control vertical reflections.

- Corners: If you have leftover materials, create bass traps by mounting panels in the corners where low-frequency buildup often occurs.

Step 7: Test Your Room

After installing your DIY acoustic panels, test the acoustics of your room. Play back some reference tracks and listen for improvements in clarity, especially in the high and mid frequencies. You should notice fewer echoes, reflections, and a more balanced sound overall.

Bonus Tips for Optimal Results:

- Use More Panels for Larger Rooms: If your space is large or highly reflective (i.e., with hardwood floors or large windows), you may need more panels to control sound adequately.

- Add Bass Traps: If you notice that your room still has excessive low-end resonance, consider adding bass traps made from the same materials but placed in the room's corners.

- Leave a Gap Between Panels and the Wall: For better absorption of lower frequencies, leave a small gap between the panel and the wall. This allows sound waves to pass through the panel more effectively.

Conclusion

MAKING YOUR OWN DIY acoustic panels is a simple and affordable way to improve the sound quality in your home studio. With a few materials and some basic tools, you can create professional-grade acoustic treatment that will help you achieve more accurate recordings and mixes. Start building your panels today and experience the difference they make in your sound!

Top 5 Essential Tips for Achieving Professional Vocal Recordings at Home

Recording vocals at home has become increasingly popular, but achieving professional sound quality can still be a challenge without the right techniques. Whether you're working in a small home studio or using minimal gear, it's possible to get high-quality results with careful attention to detail. In this blog post, we'll explore five essential tips for achieving professional vocal recordings in your home studio.

1. Create a Suitable Recording Environment

YOUR RECORDING ENVIRONMENT plays a major role in the quality of your vocal recordings. Uncontrolled reflections, room noise, or external sounds can negatively affect your vocal track. A dry, quiet space allows you to capture vocals with clarity and prevents unwanted noise from making its way into the recording.

How to Improve Your Recording Space:
- Use acoustic treatment: Invest in some foam panels, bass traps, or blankets to absorb reflections and improve sound clarity.
- Record in a small, quiet room: A walk-in closet filled with clothes can be a surprisingly effective vocal booth!
- Use a reflection filter: Portable vocal booths or reflection filters help minimize room sound by isolating the microphone from reflections.

2. Choose the Right Microphone and Positioning

SELECTING THE RIGHT microphone and placing it correctly can make a huge difference in your vocal recording quality. Condenser microphones are ideal for capturing the nuances of a vocal performance due to their sensitivity and frequency response.

Key Tips for Microphone Selection and Placement:

- Use a quality condenser microphone: This is a popular choice for vocal recording because of its clarity and detail.

- Position the mic properly: Place the microphone about 6–12 inches from the singer's mouth. A pop filter can help maintain this distance and reduce plosive sounds (like "P" and "B").

- Avoid directly pointing the mic at the singer's mouth: Pointing slightly off-axis can reduce harshness while still capturing a full sound.

3. Control Plosives and Sibilance

PLOSIVES (THE BURST of air from letters like "P" and "B") and sibilance (the harsh "S" sounds) can ruin an otherwise great vocal take. These are common issues in home recordings, but they can be controlled with the right tools and techniques.

How to Avoid Plosives and Sibilance:

- Use a pop filter: This simple, affordable tool helps minimize plosives by acting as a barrier between your singer and the mic.

- Record off-axis: By slightly angling the microphone away from the singer's mouth, you can reduce both plosives and sibilance.

- Control sibilance in post-production: If sibilance remains an issue, use a de-esser plugin during mixing to soften those harsh frequencies.

4. Monitor and Adjust Input Levels

SETTING THE CORRECT input level is critical for capturing clean, dynamic vocals. If the input is too high, you risk clipping and distortion. If it's too low, your recording will be noisy, requiring more post-processing to boost volume.

How to Set Proper Input Levels:

- Watch your levels: Aim to keep the input level peaking between -6 dB and -3 dB. This gives you enough headroom to avoid distortion.

- Avoid peaking: If you see the level meter hit 0 dB (red), reduce the gain on your audio interface or preamp to prevent clipping.

- Monitor in real-time: Always wear headphones to catch any issues like distortion, plosives, or unwanted background noise during the recording session.

5. Use Vocal Compression and EQ Wisely

EVEN WITH A GREAT RAW recording, some processing can help polish your vocals and make them sit better in a mix. Compression and EQ are two essential tools to achieve a balanced, professional vocal sound.

How to Apply Compression and EQ for Vocals:

- Compression: Use compression to smooth out the dynamic range, ensuring that louder parts don't overwhelm and quieter parts don't get lost. Start with a ratio around 3:1 or 4:1, and adjust the threshold so that only the loudest parts of the vocal are compressed.

- EQ: Roll off unnecessary low-end frequencies (below 80–100 Hz) to reduce rumble or mic stand noise. Boost around 2–5 kHz to bring out clarity and presence, and cut any harsh frequencies in the 6–10 kHz range if needed.

- Use subtle effects: Adding a bit of reverb or delay can give the vocal more space and depth, but keep these effects subtle to avoid drowning the vocal in the mix.

Final Thoughts

ACHIEVING PROFESSIONAL-sounding vocal recordings at home is entirely possible with the right techniques and a bit of practice. By creating an optimized recording environment, using proper microphone placement, controlling unwanted noises, managing input levels, and applying the right post-processing, you can capture high-quality vocals that shine in your productions. With these tips, your home recordings will sound cleaner, more polished, and ready for any mix.

6 Easy Methods to Connect an Audio Mixer to Your Computer for Mac and PC Users

Whether you're recording music, producing podcasts, or livestreaming, connecting an audio mixer to your computer is essential for better control over sound quality and inputs. Fortunately, it's easier than ever to link your audio mixer to your computer, whether you're using a Mac or PC.

Here are six simple methods you can use to connect your audio mixer to a computer for seamless audio production:

1. Using a USB Audio Interface

ONE OF THE MOST RELIABLE and efficient ways to connect your audio mixer to a computer is through a USB audio interface. A USB audio interface converts the analog signal from your mixer into a digital signal that your computer can understand, providing high-quality audio transmission.

- What You'll Need: A USB audio interface and appropriate cables (XLR, 1/4" jacks).

- How to Connect:

1. Connect the output of your mixer (usually the main or control room output) to the input of your USB audio interface.

2. Connect the USB interface to your computer via a USB cable.

3. Install the necessary drivers (if required) for your interface to work on your computer.

4. Select the audio interface as the input and output device in your DAW (Digital Audio Workstation) or audio settings.

This method is ideal for high-quality recording and gives you better control over your audio inputs and outputs.

2. Using the Mixer's Built-In USB Output

SOME MODERN AUDIO MIXERS come with a built-in USB output, making it incredibly simple to connect directly to a computer. These mixers have onboard USB interfaces that convert analog audio to digital signals.

- What You'll Need: An audio mixer with a built-in USB output and a USB cable.
- How to Connect:
1. Plug one end of the USB cable into the mixer's USB output.
2. Plug the other end into your computer's USB port.
3. Your computer should automatically recognize the mixer as an audio input/output device.
4. Choose the mixer as your input/output device in your audio settings or DAW.

This is the easiest method if your mixer supports it and is perfect for recording music, podcasts, and livestreaming.

3. Using the Line-In on Your Computer

IF YOU HAVE AN OLDER computer with a line-in input (usually a 3.5mm jack), you can connect your mixer directly to your computer without a USB interface.

- What You'll Need: A stereo 3.5mm to dual 1/4" (or RCA) cable.
- How to Connect:
1. Connect the main output of your mixer to the line-in input on your computer using the appropriate cable.
2. Open your computer's sound settings, and select the line-in as your input device.
3. Adjust the volume on your mixer to ensure the audio level is not too high or too low.

4. In your DAW or recording software, select the line-in as the input source.

While this method is easy, it may result in lower audio quality compared to using a USB audio interface.

4. Using a 3.5mm Audio Jack (For Microphone Inputs)

IF YOUR COMPUTER HAS a microphone input (common in older PCs and laptops), you can connect your mixer through this port using a suitable cable. This method is similar to using a line-in port but often results in mono audio recording.

- What You'll Need: A 1/4" to 3.5mm TRS cable or an adapter.

- How to Connect:

1. Connect your mixer's output to the microphone input using the TRS cable or adapter.

2. Adjust your mixer's output volume to avoid overloading the microphone input.

3. Set the input device to "microphone" in your computer's audio settings or DAW.

4. Test and adjust levels as needed.

This method is simple but often results in less control over audio quality and mono recording, as microphone inputs are not typically designed for high-quality stereo recording.

5. Using an RCA-to-USB Converter

IF YOUR MIXER ONLY has RCA outputs, you can use an RCA-to-USB converter to connect the mixer to your computer. RCA outputs are commonly used for consumer audio devices like DJ mixers.

- What You'll Need: An RCA-to-USB converter and an RCA cable.

- How to Connect:

1. Connect the RCA cables from your mixer's output to the RCA inputs on the converter.

2. Plug the USB end of the converter into your computer.

3. Install any necessary drivers or software for the converter.

4. Select the converter as your audio input in your computer's settings or DAW.

This method is ideal if your mixer has only RCA outputs and you need a simple solution to connect it to your computer.

6. Using a Bluetooth Audio Transmitter (For Wireless Connection)

FOR A WIRELESS SETUP, you can use a Bluetooth audio transmitter to send the mixer's audio signal to your computer.

- What You'll Need: A Bluetooth audio transmitter and a mixer with compatible outputs (RCA, 1/4", XLR).

- How to Connect:

1. Connect the Bluetooth transmitter to your mixer's output.

2. Pair the transmitter with your computer's Bluetooth receiver.

3. Select the Bluetooth device as your input/output audio source in your computer's settings or DAW.

While this method is convenient for eliminating cables, it may introduce some latency and is not ideal for high-quality recording.

Conclusion

CONNECTING YOUR AUDIO mixer to your computer can dramatically enhance your recordings and overall audio production workflow. Whether you're using a USB audio interface, a direct USB connection, or other methods, you can find a solution that works for your setup. For professional sound, using a dedicated USB interface or mixer with a built-in USB port is highly recommended. However, for simple setups or livestreams, using line-ins or Bluetooth connections may work just fine.

Choose the method that suits your setup, and enjoy improved audio quality in your productions!

Beginner's Guide to Recording Professional Voiceovers for YouTube Videos

If you're creating YouTube content, adding high-quality voiceovers can significantly enhance your videos' professionalism and appeal. Whether it's for tutorials, vlogs, or product reviews, a crisp, clear voiceover helps communicate your message effectively and keeps your audience engaged. In this beginner's guide, we'll cover everything you need to know to record professional-sounding voiceovers for your YouTube videos—even from home.

Why Voiceover Quality Matters

YOUR VOICEOVER IS A key element in capturing and holding your audience's attention. Poor sound quality—whether it's from background noise, distortion, or muffled vocals—can quickly turn viewers away. High-quality voiceovers ensure that your message is clear, professional, and easy to listen to, making your content stand out.

Step-by-Step Guide to Recording Professional Voiceovers

1. CHOOSE THE RIGHT Microphone

The microphone you use plays a big role in the quality of your voiceover recordings. Here are three common types of microphones to consider:

- USB Microphones: These are user-friendly, plug-and-play devices perfect for beginners. Simply connect them to your computer via USB, and you're ready to record. Popular choices include the Blue Yeti and Audio-Technica AT2020USB+.

- XLR Microphones: For higher sound quality, XLR microphones offer more professional results. However, they require an audio interface to connect to your computer. The Shure SM7B and Rode NT1-A are excellent options for more serious creators.

- Lavalier Microphones: If you prefer a less intrusive setup, lavalier (clip-on) microphones can capture clear voice recordings for videos where you move around or record on-camera.

For beginners, a USB microphone is a great choice due to its ease of use and affordability.

2. Set Up Your Recording Environment

To achieve clean and professional voiceovers, you need to minimize unwanted background noise. You don't need a full recording studio, but some simple steps can make a big difference:

- Quiet space: Choose a room that is quiet, away from household noise, traffic, or other distractions. Close windows and doors to block out external sounds.

- Acoustic treatment: If possible, add soft furnishings or sound-absorbing materials (like foam panels or blankets) to reduce echo and room reverb. Even a closet full of clothes can work as an effective sound booth!

- Turn off devices: Make sure to turn off or silence any electronic devices, such as fans, phones, or computers, that could create background noise.

3. Position Your Microphone Correctly

The placement of your microphone impacts the clarity and tone of your voice recording. Here's how to position it for optimal results:

- Distance: Place the microphone about 6-12 inches away from your mouth. If you're using a pop filter (recommended to reduce plosive sounds like "p" and "b"), position the filter between the mic and your mouth.

- Angle: Slightly angle the microphone to avoid directly facing it. This helps minimize breath and mouth sounds that can ruin a clean recording.

- Pop Filter: Use a pop filter to reduce popping noises from plosive sounds, especially if you're using a condenser microphone.

4. Select Recording Software (DAW)

A DAW (Digital Audio Workstation) is the software you'll use to record, edit, and enhance your voiceover. There are many options, but here are some beginner-friendly ones:

- Audacity: Free and simple to use, Audacity is a popular DAW for voiceover recordings. It has all the basic features you need to record, edit, and clean up your audio.

- Adobe Audition: A more advanced (and paid) option, Adobe Audition offers a range of professional tools for recording and editing voiceovers.

- GarageBand: If you're on a Mac, GarageBand is a free and intuitive choice with solid audio recording features.

Choose a DAW that fits your needs and experience level.

5. Recording Your Voiceover

Now that your setup is ready, it's time to hit record. Here are a few tips to ensure your voiceover sounds professional:

- Warm-up: Warm up your voice before recording to reduce strain and improve clarity. Simple exercises like humming, lip trills, or reading a paragraph out loud can help loosen your vocal cords.

- Speak clearly: Articulate your words clearly and maintain a natural tone. Speak as if you're talking to a friend, but with added clarity and intention.

- Stay consistent: Try to maintain consistent volume levels throughout your recording. Speak at a moderate pace, avoiding the temptation to rush through sentences.

6. Edit and Enhance Your Recording

After recording your voiceover, editing is the next step to make it sound professional. Here's what to focus on:

- Noise reduction: Use your DAW's noise reduction tools to remove any background noise that may have been picked up during recording.

- EQ: Equalization (EQ) can help shape the tone of your voice by adjusting frequencies. Boost the low-mid frequencies for warmth and clarity while cutting any harsh high-end or low-end noise.

- Compression: Compression helps level out the dynamic range of your voice, ensuring that quiet parts are heard clearly and loud parts don't clip or distort.

- De-essing: De-essing reduces harsh "s" sounds that can become distracting in a recording. Most DAWs have a built-in de-esser effect.

- Add a limiter: A limiter ensures that the loudest parts of your recording don't exceed a set volume threshold, preventing distortion.

7. Export and Sync with Video

Once your voiceover is edited and polished, export the file in a high-quality format such as WAV or MP3. Next, sync the voiceover with your video in your video editing software, ensuring that the timing aligns perfectly with your visuals.

Additional Tips for Professional Voiceovers

- PRACTICE MAKES PERFECT: Like any skill, recording voiceovers takes practice. Don't worry if your first recordings aren't perfect—keep refining your technique.

- Use headphones: When editing, always use headphones to hear every detail of your recording. This helps you catch any small errors or imperfections you might miss on speakers.

- Stay hydrated: Drink plenty of water before and during your recording session to keep your voice clear and prevent vocal fatigue.

Conclusion

Recording professional voiceovers for your YouTube videos doesn't require an expensive studio—just the right tools, setup, and technique. By choosing a quality microphone, setting up your recording space, and mastering a few editing basics, you can achieve studio-quality voiceovers that will elevate your content and keep your audience engaged.

With these tips, you'll be well on your way to producing clear, captivating voiceovers that enhance your YouTube videos and take your content to the next level!

Essential Components for a Beginners Home Studio Setup

Starting your own home studio can be an exciting journey for any musician or producer. Whether you're recording vocals, playing instruments, or producing beats, a well-equipped home studio is key to capturing great sound. Setting up a studio doesn't need to be expensive or overly complex—getting the basics right can take you a long way. Here are the essential components you need to kickstart your home studio setup as a beginner.

1. Computer or Laptop

THE HEART OF YOUR HOME studio is your computer. Whether you prefer using a desktop or a laptop, you'll need a machine that can handle the demands of music production software. Most modern computers will work fine, but aim for something with a fast processor (Intel i5 or higher) and at least 8GB of RAM to ensure smooth performance.

- Tip: If you're serious about producing music, invest in more RAM (16GB or higher) and a solid-state drive (SSD) for faster file processing and loading times.

2. Digital Audio Workstation (DAW)

A DAW IS THE SOFTWARE that allows you to record, edit, and mix your music. Some popular options include:
- GarageBand (for Mac users) – beginner-friendly and free.
- Ableton Live – great for both live performances and studio production.
- FL Studio – excellent for electronic music and beat making.

- Logic Pro X – more advanced but packed with professional features.
- Pro Tools – the industry standard for professional music production.

Choose a DAW that fits your style and offers the features you need.

3. Audio Interface

AN AUDIO INTERFACE allows you to connect your instruments, microphones, and speakers to your computer. It converts analog signals (like guitar or vocals) into digital signals that your computer can process.

- Tip: Look for an audio interface with at least two inputs (so you can record vocals and an instrument simultaneously) and one or two headphone outputs. Popular beginner interfaces include the Focusrite Scarlett 2i2 or the PreSonus AudioBox.

4. Studio Monitors

STUDIO MONITORS ARE speakers designed specifically for music production, offering a flat, accurate frequency response. Unlike consumer speakers, which often color the sound (boosting bass or treble), studio monitors provide an unaltered representation of your recordings.

- Tip: Look for affordable monitors like Yamaha HS5 or KRK Rokit 5, which offer great sound quality for beginners.

5. Studio Headphones

WHILE STUDIO MONITORS are ideal for mixing, studio headphones are essential for detailed listening and late-night sessions. You'll want closed-back headphones for recording (to prevent sound bleed into the mic) and open-back headphones for mixing (for a more natural sound).

- Tip: The Audio-Technica ATH-M50X or the Sony MDR-7506 are popular options known for their clarity and comfort.

6. Microphone

A GOOD MICROPHONE IS crucial for recording vocals and instruments. For beginners, a condenser microphone is a great all-round option because it's sensitive and captures a broad frequency range, making it ideal for vocals and acoustic instruments.

- Tip: Consider the Audio-Technica AT2020 or Rode NT1-A as budget-friendly but high-quality options.

7. MIDI Controller

IF YOU PLAN ON PRODUCING electronic music or adding virtual instruments to your tracks, a MIDI controller is a must. MIDI controllers allow you to play software instruments in your DAW using a keyboard or drum pads.

- Tip: The Novation Launchkey Mini or Akai MPK Mini are compact, beginner-friendly MIDI controllers with easy-to-use features.

8. Pop Filter

A POP FILTER IS A SIMPLE yet effective tool that prevents harsh plosive sounds (like "p" and "b") from ruining your vocal recordings. It's placed in front of the microphone to soften bursts of air from the vocalist.

- Tip: You don't need to spend much on a pop filter. Basic models are affordable and get the job done well.

9. Microphone Stand

HAVING A STABLE MICROPHONE stand is essential for keeping your mic in place while recording. Adjustable stands are recommended to accommodate different recording situations, whether you're standing, sitting, or playing an instrument.
    - Tip: The K&M Microphone Stand is durable, adjustable, and perfect for home studio use.

10. Cables

GOOD QUALITY XLR CABLES for your microphone and TRS/TS cables for your instruments are vital to ensure a clean, noise-free signal. Always have a few spare cables on hand in case one breaks or becomes faulty.
    - Tip: Invest in durable cables from reputable brands like Mogami or Planet Waves to avoid signal interference.

11. Acoustic Treatment

SOUNDPROOFING YOUR room is key to achieving high-quality recordings and mixes. Bare walls and reflective surfaces can cause unwanted echoes and muddy sound. Start with some basic acoustic panels or bass traps to absorb sound and prevent reflections.
    - Tip: You can also make DIY acoustic panels for a budget-friendly option (check out our DIY guide for more information).

12. External Hard Drive

RECORDING AND PRODUCING music takes up a lot of storage space. An external hard drive is essential for backing up your projects, sound libraries, and samples to prevent data loss.

- Tip: Choose a SSD external drive for faster file transfers. Brands like Samsung and SanDisk offer reliable options.

Conclusion

WITH THESE ESSENTIAL components, you'll have a strong foundation for building your home studio. Start with the basics, and as your skills and budget grow, you can expand your gear to suit your evolving needs. Remember, it's not about having the most expensive equipment; it's about making the most of what you have and creating great music from the comfort of your own space. Happy recording!

Advanced Drum Programming Techniques for Creating Irresistible Grooves in Your Tracks

A powerful groove is the backbone of any great track. Whether you're producing electronic music, hip-hop, pop, or rock, the quality of your drum programming can elevate your entire song. Advanced drum programming techniques give you the edge you need to create grooves that captivate listeners, keep them moving, and leave a lasting impression. Let's dive into some expert techniques to take your drum programming to the next level.

1. Layering for Richer Drums

LAYERING DIFFERENT drum samples is an effective way to add depth and complexity to your grooves. By stacking different kicks, snares, or hi-hats, you can create a unique sound that has more character and energy.

- Tip: Combine a low, sub-heavy kick with a punchier, mid-range kick to cover the full frequency spectrum. Experiment with layering snares, adding a clap or a snare with more texture to fill out the sound. Adjust the levels of each layer to ensure balance, and use EQ to carve out frequencies so the layers complement each other.

2. Varying Velocity for a Human Touch

REAL DRUMS ARE NEVER hit with the exact same force every time. By varying the velocity (how hard or soft each hit is) in your MIDI drum patterns, you can simulate this human element and make your grooves feel more natural and less robotic.

- Tip: Use lower velocity values for off-beat hits or ghost notes, and increase velocity for accents, like the first beat of each measure. This subtle variation adds dynamics and energy, making your drum patterns feel alive.

3. Off-Grid Programming for Groove

PERFECTLY QUANTIZED beats can sound sterile. Introducing slight timing deviations can give your drums a more organic and groove-driven feel. This is particularly effective in genres like hip-hop, funk, and electronic music.

- Tip: Try shifting some snare or hi-hat hits slightly off the grid (a technique known as "swing" or "shuffle"). This small change can make a huge difference in how your groove feels. Adjust the swing amount to match the vibe of your track, and use it sparingly to avoid throwing off the rhythm too much.

4. Incorporating Triplets and Syncopation

TRIPLETS AND SYNCOPATION add complexity and intrigue to your drum patterns. They break the predictable flow of a 4/4 beat and create rhythmic tension that draws listeners in.

- Tip: Experiment with triplet hi-hat patterns or syncopated kick drum hits. These patterns can create a more intricate and compelling groove, especially when combined with simpler elements in other parts of the track. Syncopation adds rhythmic "surprises" that keep the listener engaged.

5. Using Ghost Notes for Texture

GHOST NOTES ARE QUIETER, subtler hits that sit in between your main drum hits, adding texture and nuance to your groove. They're especially effective when used with snares or toms.
   - Tip: Add ghost snare notes at low velocity between your primary snare hits. This can create a shuffle effect or add depth to a basic pattern. Similarly, using ghost hi-hat hits can make your hi-hat patterns feel more dynamic and less repetitive.

6. Playing with Polyrhythms

POLYRHYTHMS ARE WHEN two or more conflicting rhythms are played simultaneously. This technique can give your drum patterns a complex, layered feel that stands out from traditional beats.
   - Tip: Start by adding a different time signature to one percussion element. For example, keep your kick and snare in 4/4, but program a hi-hat pattern in 3/4 or 5/4. While this might sound chaotic at first, when done right, it can create an interesting rhythmic tension that pushes your track forward.

7. Automation for Dynamic Drums

AUTOMATION ALLOWS YOU to make real-time changes to parameters like volume, pitch, panning, and effects. This keeps your drum track evolving throughout the song and prevents it from feeling stagnant.
   - Tip: Automate volume changes on your hi-hats or cymbals to create intensity during different sections of the song. You can also automate reverb to increase on specific snare hits or use pitch automation to create subtle pitch shifts in your kick drums. This adds movement and excitement to your track.

8. Creative Use of Effects

EFFECTS LIKE REVERB, delay, distortion, and modulation can add unique character to your drum sounds. But instead of slapping effects on every element, think strategically about where and when to use them.

- Tip: Apply reverb sparingly to certain snares or claps to add space and depth without muddying the mix. Use subtle delay on hi-hats to create a bouncing, syncopated effect. For more aggressive tracks, experiment with distortion on your kick drums to add grit and intensity.

9. Automation for Build-ups and Transitions

DRUM FILLS, TRANSITIONS, and build-ups are crucial for maintaining the flow of your song and adding tension before drops or chorus sections.

- Tip: Use automation to gradually increase reverb or delay as you approach a drop. You can also automate the speed of a drum roll or apply a high-pass filter to progressively thin out your kick or snare before bringing it back in full force. This helps create a natural build-up and enhances the impact of transitions.

10. Experiment with Unconventional Percussion

DON'T LIMIT YOURSELF to traditional drum sounds. Incorporating unique, unconventional percussion elements can add creativity and make your track stand out.

- Tip: Experiment with foley sounds, such as hitting household objects, rustling paper, or tapping glass. Layer these organic sounds with your main drums for added texture. Percussion instruments like tambourines, bongos, or shakers can also add a fresh rhythmic feel to your track.

Conclusion

MASTERING ADVANCED drum programming techniques is key to creating grooves that are both engaging and irresistible. By layering samples, introducing subtle timing variations, using syncopation and ghost notes, and creatively applying effects, you can transform a basic beat into a dynamic, living groove. Experiment with these techniques, listen to how they interact with your track, and watch your music come alive with captivating rhythms that listeners can't resist.

Step-by-Step Guide to Properly Restringing an Acoustic Guitar for Optimal Sound and Playability

Restringing your acoustic guitar is essential for maintaining its sound quality and playability. Over time, guitar strings lose their brightness, become harder to tune, and can affect your overall performance. In this guide, we'll walk you through the steps to properly restring your acoustic guitar, ensuring it stays in top shape.

Step 1: Gather Your Tools

BEFORE YOU BEGIN, MAKE sure you have the following tools:
  - A new set of acoustic guitar strings (choose the gauge that best suits your style).
  - A string winder (optional but speeds up the process).
  - A wire cutter to trim excess string.
  - A tuner for accurate tuning after restringing.
  - A soft cloth for cleaning your guitar while the strings are off.

Step 2: Remove the Old Strings

START BY LOOSENING the tension on each string:
  - Use a string winder (or manually turn the tuning pegs) to loosen the strings until they're slack.
  - Once they are loose enough, unwind the strings from the tuning pegs.
  - Carefully remove the bridge pins (the pegs at the bottom of the guitar holding the strings in place). You can use the notch on your string winder or pliers to gently pull them out.

After removing the bridge pins, the strings will slip out of the bridge, and you can remove them from the tuning pegs. Discard the old strings.

Step 3: Clean Your Guitar

WITH THE STRINGS REMOVED, it's the perfect time to clean your guitar:

- Use a soft, dry cloth to wipe down the fretboard, body, and bridge of your guitar. This removes dirt and oils that have accumulated during playing.

- For deeper cleaning, you can use a dedicated fretboard cleaner and conditioner, especially if your fretboard is made of rosewood or ebony.

Step 4: Install the New Strings

NOW THAT YOUR GUITAR is clean, it's time to install your new strings.

1. Insert the Strings into the Bridge:

- Start with the low E string (the thickest string). Insert the ball end of the string into the hole in the bridge and place the bridge pin back in, pushing down gently while pulling up on the string to lock it in place.

- Repeat this process for the remaining strings, working from the low E string to the high E string.

2. String the Tuning Pegs:

- Take the other end of the low E string and thread it through the hole in the tuning peg. Leave about 2–3 inches of slack for winding.

- Turn the tuning peg in a clockwise direction to tighten the string. Ensure that the string wraps neatly around the peg without overlapping, which improves tuning stability.

- Use a string winder for speed and continue turning until the string is snug (but not fully tightened).

3. Repeat for All Strings:

- Work your way through all the strings, repeating the same process for each: insert the ball end into the bridge, secure the bridge pin, and wind the string on the corresponding tuning peg.

- Wind the lower three strings (E, A, D) in a clockwise direction and the higher three strings (G, B, high E) in a counterclockwise direction to match the tuning pegs.

Step 5: Tune Your Guitar

ONCE ALL THE STRINGS are installed, it's time to tune your guitar:

- Use a guitar tuner to accurately tune each string to the correct pitch: E, A, D, G, B, E (from lowest to highest).

- After initial tuning, stretch the strings gently by pulling them upward a few times. This helps settle the strings and prevents them from going out of tune quickly.

- Retune your guitar after stretching, as the strings will loosen slightly.

Step 6: Trim the Excess String

NOW THAT YOUR GUITAR is tuned, use wire cutters to trim the excess string at the tuning pegs. Leave about 1/4 inch of string at the end for a neat finish.

Step 7: Play and Re-Tune

AFTER RESTRINGING, your new strings may take some time to fully settle. Play your guitar for a few minutes, then re-tune as necessary.

New strings tend to stretch during the first few hours of play, so regular tuning adjustments will help keep your guitar sounding its best.

Final Thoughts

PROPERLY RESTRINGING your acoustic guitar can dramatically improve its sound and playability. By following this step-by-step guide, you'll ensure that your guitar maintains optimal tone and tuning stability. With clean strings and careful attention to detail, your guitar will feel fresh, sound vibrant, and be ready for your next performance or practice session.

How to Use Vocal EQ Zones to Instantly Improve Your Voice in Recordings

Achieving a professional vocal sound in recordings often comes down to using EQ (equalization) effectively. EQ allows you to shape your vocals, enhance clarity, remove unwanted frequencies, and ensure your voice sits perfectly in the mix. By understanding the different vocal EQ zones, you can make precise adjustments that instantly improve your voice in recordings.

In this blog post, we'll break down the essential EQ zones and provide tips on how to use them to enhance your voice.

What Are Vocal EQ Zones?

EQ ZONES REFER TO SPECIFIC frequency ranges in your vocal recording that affect different aspects of the voice. These zones help you target certain characteristics of your vocals, such as brightness, warmth, and presence. The main EQ zones for vocals generally fall into the following categories:

- Sub-Bass (20–80 Hz)
- Low Mids (100–300 Hz)
- Midrange (300–1,000 Hz)
- High Mids (1,000–5,000 Hz)
- Presence (5,000–8,000 Hz)
- Air (8,000–20,000 Hz)

Step-by-Step Guide to Using Vocal EQ Zones

1. SUB-BASS (20–80 Hz): Cleaning Up Unwanted Low Frequencies

The sub-bass zone contains very low frequencies that are rarely useful for vocals. In fact, too much sub-bass can make your vocals sound muddy and indistinct.

- Action: Use a high-pass filter to remove everything below 80 Hz. This helps clean up any low-end rumble or unwanted noise while keeping your vocal recording clean and clear. Be careful not to cut too high, as this may thin out your voice too much.

2. Low Mids (100–300 Hz): Adding Warmth or Reducing Muddiness

The low mids are where the body of your voice lives. While this range can add warmth and fullness to your vocals, it's also the zone that can easily become muddy or boomy.

- Action: If your vocals sound too thin, you can boost gently around 150–250 Hz to add warmth. On the other hand, if your voice feels too muddy, you can slightly reduce frequencies in this range to clear things up. Don't overdo it, as cutting too much will make your vocals lose richness.

3. Midrange (300–1,000 Hz): Controlling Nasality and Boxiness

The midrange is crucial for vocal clarity, but too much energy in this zone can make your voice sound nasal or boxy. This is where a lot of vocal definition happens, but it's also an area that can build up unwanted resonances.

- Action: If your voice sounds too nasally, try a slight cut around 600–800 Hz. Conversely, if you need more clarity and presence, you can add a slight boost around 400–600 Hz. Be careful with this zone, as boosting or cutting too much can drastically change the character of your voice.

4. High Mids (1,000–5,000 Hz): Adding Intelligibility and Crispness

The high mids are where much of the vocal intelligibility and crispness resides. Boosting this area can make your vocals cut through a dense mix, but overdoing it can cause harshness and fatigue for listeners.

- Action: Boost between 2,000–4,000 Hz to add clarity and help the voice stand out in the mix. Be subtle with your boosts here, as too much can make your vocals sound shrill or harsh. If your vocals are too sharp, you can cut slightly in this range to reduce harshness.

5. Presence (5,000–8,000 Hz): Enhancing Brightness and Definition

The presence zone is where your vocals gain brightness and definition. This area can make your vocals sparkle and bring them to the forefront of a track. It's especially useful for pop, R&B, or any style where clear, bright vocals are important.

- Action: A slight boost between 5,000–7,000 Hz can give your voice that polished, professional sound. This helps add airiness and clarity, but be cautious—boosting too much can make your voice sound brittle or overly sharp.

6. Air (8,000–20,000 Hz): Adding Shine and Airiness

The air zone is the top-end frequencies that can add a sense of openness and "air" to your vocal recording. This range is especially important for female vocals or high-pitched voices, as it adds a soft sparkle without overpowering the mix.

- Action: Apply a gentle boost above 10,000 Hz for a smooth, airy finish to your vocals. This will make your recordings sound more polished and professional. Be careful, though—over-boosting this range can introduce hiss or other high-frequency noise.

Bonus Tips for EQing Vocals

- ALWAYS A/B TEST: AFTER making adjustments, compare your EQ changes by toggling the effect on and off. This ensures you're making improvements rather than degrading the overall sound.

- Use Reference Tracks: Listen to professionally mixed vocals in your genre to understand how they're balanced across the frequency spectrum. This can help guide your EQ decisions.

- Use a Spectrum Analyzer: Visual tools like spectrum analyzers can help you see where frequencies are building up in your vocals. Use this tool to spot problematic areas and make more informed EQ adjustments.

- EQ in Context: Always EQ your vocals in the context of the full mix. What sounds great in solo may not sit well once all the instruments are in place. Make sure your vocal EQ complements the other elements of the track.

Final Thoughts

BY UNDERSTANDING AND mastering vocal EQ zones, you can dramatically improve the quality of your recordings. Each frequency range plays a unique role in shaping your vocal tone, and knowing how to adjust these zones can help you create polished, professional-sounding vocals. Whether you're looking to add warmth, clarity, or brightness to your voice, EQ is a powerful tool that can make an immediate impact on your sound.

Step-by-Step Guide to Learning Any Synthesizer: Essential Tips for Beginners and Pros

Learning how to use a synthesizer can feel overwhelming at first, but with the right approach, it becomes an exciting journey of sound exploration. Whether you're a beginner looking to dive into synths for the first time or an experienced musician wanting to refine your skills, understanding the fundamentals and working through key steps can help you master any synthesizer. This *Guide to Learning Any Synthesizer* offers a step-by-step breakdown to help you build a solid foundation and grow your synth expertise.

Step 1: Understand the Basics of Sound Synthesis

BEFORE JUMPING INTO a synthesizer, it's important to grasp the basic principles of sound synthesis. Synthesizers create sound by manipulating audio signals in various ways, and knowing these fundamental concepts will make the rest of your learning experience easier.

Key Concepts to Know:

- Oscillators (OSC): These generate the basic waveforms that are the starting point of most synth sounds. Common waveforms include sine, square, triangle, and sawtooth, each having a distinct tone and character.

- Filters (VCF): Filters shape the sound by removing or emphasizing certain frequencies. The most common is the low-pass filter, which cuts high frequencies, making the sound warmer or darker.

- Envelopes (ADSR): Envelopes control how a sound evolves over time, including Attack (how quickly the sound reaches its peak),

Decay, Sustain (the level the sound holds while a key is pressed), and Release (how quickly the sound fades after the key is released).

- LFO (Low-Frequency Oscillator): LFOs modulate various parameters like pitch, filter cutoff, or volume, adding motion and depth to the sound.

Step 2: Familiarize Yourself with the Interface

EACH SYNTHESIZER, WHETHER software or hardware, has a unique layout. Spend some time getting to know the layout of your particular synth. Understanding where things are located on the interface will save you time and allow you to dive deeper into sound creation.

How to Get Started:

- Identify key sections: Most synths have sections like Oscillators, Filters, Envelopes, and Modulation. Start by familiarizing yourself with where these are located.

- Check out presets: Most synthesizers come with pre-made sounds or presets. Use these as a way to explore how the synth works, and examine the settings used to create these sounds.

- Label important controls: If your synth allows for custom labeling or notes, make reminders of what certain knobs or sliders do, especially when learning a more complex interface.

Step 3: Experiment with Basic Presets

MANY SYNTHESIZERS COME with a wide variety of presets. While your ultimate goal may be to design your own sounds, presets are a great starting point for understanding how specific parameters affect sound.

Steps for Experimentation:

- Choose a simple preset: Start with a basic sound, like a clean sine wave or a pad, and begin tweaking different controls like the filter cutoff or LFO rate.

- Analyze the settings: Compare the settings on different presets to see how changing parameters (oscillators, filters, effects) alters the sound.

- Modify presets: Once you're familiar with the basics, try making small adjustments to the presets to see how they change. For example, increase the attack to make the sound fade in slowly, or add more resonance to the filter for a sharper, more focused tone.

Step 4: Learn to Create Your Own Sound from Scratch

ONCE YOU'VE GOTTEN comfortable with presets, the next step is creating your own sounds from scratch. Start with a blank slate by initializing the synth (resetting all settings) and build your sound one element at a time.

Steps for Sound Design:

- Start with a single oscillator: Choose a waveform (sine, saw, square, etc.) and listen to how it sounds by itself. Experiment with adding other oscillators or tuning them slightly apart for a richer tone.

- Add filtering: Use the filter section to shape the sound. A low-pass filter can soften a harsh waveform, while a high-pass filter can thin out a sound to make it fit better in a mix.

- Use envelopes for dynamics: Set the envelope to control how the sound evolves. For example, a short attack will make a punchy sound, while a long release will create a more ambient, sustaining tone.

- Experiment with modulation: Add movement by applying an LFO to parameters like pitch or filter cutoff. This can add subtle wobble or dramatic sweeps, depending on the settings.

Step 5: Explore Modulation and Effects

MODULATION AND EFFECTS can take your sounds to the next level by adding complexity, movement, and texture.

Modulation Tips:

- LFO to Pitch: Modulating the pitch of an oscillator can create vibrato or a more extreme wobble effect. Adjust the rate and depth to find the sweet spot for your sound.

- LFO to Filter Cutoff: This can make your sound sweep in and out, which is great for rhythmic effects or evolving pads.

- Envelope to Filter: By routing an envelope to a filter, you can control how the filter opens or closes over time, creating a dynamic sound that changes as you play.

Effects Tips:

- Reverb: Add space to your sound with reverb to give it depth and atmosphere. A short reverb works well for rhythmic sounds, while a long reverb can turn a simple sound into an epic ambient wash.

- Delay: Use delay to create echoes that add texture and rhythmic interest.

- Chorus: Apply chorus to thicken up your sound by slightly detuning multiple versions of the same signal, creating a lush, wide stereo effect.

Step 6: Use Arpeggiators and Sequencers

MANY SYNTHESIZERS INCLUDE arpeggiators and sequencers, which can be powerful tools for creating rhythmic patterns and melodies.

How to Use Arpeggiators:

- Activate the arpeggiator: This will automatically play the notes of a chord in a repeating pattern. Experiment with different arpeggio styles (up, down, random) and tempos.

- Adjust the rate: Changing the speed of the arpeggiator can create different feels, from slow, evolving soundscapes to fast, energetic riffs.

Sequencer Tips:

- Program simple patterns: Start by programming a basic sequence of notes and tweak the timing, velocity, or pitch to add variation.

- Sync with tempo: Many synths allow you to sync the sequencer with your DAW's tempo, making it easy to integrate the sequence into your production.

Step 7: Practice with Purpose

LIKE LEARNING ANY INSTRUMENT, mastering a synthesizer takes time and practice. Set aside regular practice sessions where you focus on specific aspects of the synth.

Practice Tips:

- Focus on one section at a time: One day, practice working only with oscillators; another day, focus on filters or modulation. This approach helps you master each component before moving on.

- Recreate sounds: Listen to your favorite songs and try to recreate the synth sounds you hear. This is a great way to apply your knowledge and understand how different settings work together.

- Keep experimenting: Synthesis is an art form, so don't be afraid to push boundaries and create unconventional sounds. The more you experiment, the more confident you'll become.

Final Thoughts

LEARNING HOW TO USE any synthesizer is both a technical and creative journey. By understanding the fundamentals of sound synthesis, experimenting with presets, and diving into modulation and effects, you can unlock a world of sonic possibilities. Whether you're a beginner or a seasoned pro, this step-by-step guide will help you gain the skills you need to confidently design and manipulate sounds with any synthesizer. Keep exploring, stay curious, and let your creativity lead the way!

How to Properly Position Your Microphone for Optimal Vocal Recording: Tips for Best Results

Achieving a professional-quality vocal recording starts with proper microphone placement. Whether you're recording at home or in a studio, how you properly position your microphone can make all the difference in capturing clear, rich vocals. Poor positioning can lead to unwanted noise, distortion, or muffled sound. Follow these tips to ensure your vocal recordings sound crisp, clean, and professional.

1. Choose the Right Type of Microphone

BEFORE DIVING INTO positioning, it's essential to select the right microphone for your voice and recording environment. While positioning is key, using the wrong microphone can hinder your results regardless of placement.

Types of Microphones:

- Condenser microphones: These are the most popular for vocal recording due to their sensitivity and wide frequency range. They're ideal for capturing detailed, nuanced performances.

- Dynamic microphones: More rugged and less sensitive than condensers, dynamic mics are often used in live performances but can work well for certain vocal styles, particularly louder, more aggressive vocals.

- Ribbon microphones: These are less common but provide a warm, vintage sound, perfect for capturing smooth, soulful vocals.

2. Distance from the Microphone

ONE OF THE MOST CRITICAL factors in achieving optimal vocal recording is how far you are from the microphone. Standing too close or too far away can result in distortion, inconsistent volume, or a loss of detail.

Ideal Distance:

- 6-12 inches away from the microphone is usually the sweet spot for vocal recordings. This distance allows the mic to pick up the full range of your voice without overloading or capturing too much background noise.

- Use a pop filter: A pop filter helps control plosive sounds (like hard "P" and "B" sounds) that can cause unwanted bursts of air to hit the microphone, distorting the recording.

Pro Tips:

- For a warmer sound, move closer to the mic (6 inches), but be careful to avoid excessive proximity effect (an increase in bass response when too close to the mic).

- If you have a powerful voice or tend to project loudly, step back to about 12 inches to avoid distortion and maintain clarity.

3. Adjust the Microphone Height

THE HEIGHT AT WHICH you position the microphone relative to your mouth plays a significant role in capturing different tonal characteristics of your voice.

Height Considerations:

- Level with your mouth: Positioning the mic at the same height as your mouth produces a balanced, natural sound. This is the most common position for general vocal recording.

- Slightly above your mouth: For a brighter tone, position the mic slightly above mouth level and angle it down toward you. This captures more high-end frequencies and can result in a cleaner, crisper sound.

- Slightly below your mouth: Positioning the mic below your mouth and angling it up can result in a warmer sound. This can be helpful if you're looking to capture more of the chest resonance in your voice.

Pro Tips:

- Experiment with slight adjustments in mic height to find the sweet spot for your voice and style. Small changes can make a significant difference in the tonal quality.

- Stand up straight when recording to ensure proper vocal projection and clarity.

4. Microphone Angle and Tilt

THE ANGLE AT WHICH your microphone is positioned in relation to your mouth can affect how it captures your voice, especially when it comes to avoiding unwanted noise and plosives.

Optimal Angles:

- Straight-on position: This is the most straightforward approach, where the mic is directly facing your mouth. While this captures the most direct sound, it can also amplify sibilance (sharp "S" sounds) and plosives.

- Slight off-axis positioning: To reduce plosive and sibilant sounds, try angling the microphone slightly off-axis, so it's facing slightly above or to the side of your mouth instead of directly in front of it. This reduces the risk of harsh noises without sacrificing vocal clarity.

Pro Tips:

- A 10 to 15-degree tilt off-axis is usually enough to minimize plosives without losing the full spectrum of your voice.

- If you're recording multiple vocal takes or harmonies, try different angles to vary the tonal quality of each take.

5. Control Your Environment

WHILE PROPER MICROPHONE positioning is crucial, your recording environment also plays a significant role in achieving high-quality sound. Even the best mic placement won't fix problems caused by excessive room noise or poor acoustics.

Improve Your Recording Environment:

- Use acoustic treatment: If possible, set up your recording area with acoustic foam panels, sound blankets, or other dampening materials to reduce echo and reverb. Hard surfaces like walls and ceilings can reflect sound, leading to a less clean recording.

- Record in a quiet space: Reduce background noise by recording in a space free from distractions like fans, air conditioning, or street noise.

- Use a reflection filter: If you're recording in a less-than-ideal space, consider using a reflection filter (a small portable acoustic shield) to reduce room reflections and focus the microphone on your voice.

6. Maintain a Consistent Position While Singing

IT'S IMPORTANT TO MAINTAIN consistent positioning throughout the recording session to avoid uneven vocal levels or inconsistent sound quality.

Tips for Consistency:

- Stay centered: Keep your head aligned with the microphone and avoid moving too far to the side while singing, as this can result in a loss of clarity or create an uneven sound.

- Control your dynamics: If you're singing softly or loudly in different parts of the song, adjust your position slightly, stepping closer for softer parts and moving back for louder sections. However, make these adjustments subtle to maintain consistent mic positioning.

- Avoid excessive movement: While it's natural to move slightly when singing, try to stay relatively still to ensure consistent vocal quality. You can still express yourself, but keep the mic in mind!

Final Thoughts

PROPER MICROPHONE POSITIONING is a game-changer when it comes to vocal recording. By choosing the right distance, adjusting the height and angle, and controlling your environment, you can capture clear, professional vocals that elevate your music production. Experiment with these tips to find the optimal setup for your voice, and remember that even small adjustments can have a big impact on your sound.

Now that you have the tools to improve your vocal recordings, it's time to put them into practice and make your next project shine!

How to Create Epic Vocals Using Effects and Production Techniques Without Being a Trained Singer

You don't need to be a trained singer to create epic, standout vocals in your music. Modern production tools allow even those with minimal vocal ability to create polished, powerful, and unique vocal tracks. By using a combination of effects and creative production techniques, you can transform basic vocal recordings into something truly epic. Here's how to achieve that larger-than-life vocal sound, even without formal vocal training.

1. Autotune and Pitch Correction

AUTOTUNE IS ONE OF the most common tools used in modern music production to correct pitch issues and enhance vocal performances. If you're not a trained singer, pitch correction can help you stay in key and achieve professional results.

How to Use It:

- Subtle Pitch Correction: Set autotune to gently correct minor pitch issues without making the effect too obvious. This keeps your vocals sounding natural while correcting mistakes.

- Hard Tuning for Effect: If you're going for a more robotic, modern sound (à la T-Pain or Travis Scott), set the autotune to a faster response time, which creates the characteristic "hard tuning" effect.

- Pitch Shifting: Use pitch shifting to experiment with different octaves, creating layered harmonies or unique vocal effects that add depth and interest.

2. Layering Vocals for Thickness

ONE OF THE MOST EFFECTIVE ways to make your vocals sound epic is by layering multiple takes of the same vocal line. This gives the sound more depth and richness, which can compensate for a lack of vocal range or power.

How to Layer Vocals:

- Double Tracking: Record your vocal take multiple times and stack them together in the mix. Slight variations in each take will give the vocals a natural thickness.

- Panning Left and Right: Pan some layers slightly to the left and others to the right for a wider, fuller sound.

- Harmonies and Octaves: If possible, record a few takes in different octaves or harmonize with yourself. Even subtle differences can create a more dynamic sound.

3. Reverb and Delay for Space and Depth

REVERB AND DELAY ARE essential effects for adding space and depth to your vocals, making them sound bigger and more atmospheric. They can help you hide small imperfections while creating an epic, cinematic quality.

Using Reverb:

- Large Hall or Plate Reverbs: Use a large reverb, like a hall or plate setting, to give your vocals a lush, expansive sound. This adds a sense of grandeur and makes the vocals feel more "epic."

- Control the Reverb Tail: Adjust the decay time so that the reverb doesn't overwhelm the clarity of your vocals. A longer decay can make vocals sound more ethereal, while a shorter one keeps them crisp.

- Pre-Delay: Add a pre-delay to your reverb so that the effect kicks in slightly after the initial vocal sound, keeping the lyrics intelligible while still adding space.

Using Delay:

- Subtle Slapback Delay: A slapback delay can thicken the vocals without making the delay too noticeable. This is great for adding weight to your vocal line.

- Sync to Tempo: If you want a rhythmic effect, use a delay synced to the tempo of your track to create a repeating echo that adds a sense of movement.

4. Distortion and Saturation for Edge

DISTORTION AND SATURATION can add grit and character to vocals, making them sound more aggressive or textured. This can be especially useful for giving energy to your voice if it's lacking in natural power.

How to Apply It:

- Saturation for Warmth: Use gentle saturation to add warmth and richness to your vocals. This will give them a more analog feel and can make them stand out in the mix.

- Distortion for Grit: Apply more aggressive distortion to specific sections, like choruses or ad-libs, to give your vocals a raw, edgy sound.

- Parallel Distortion: Blend a distorted version of your vocal with the clean signal for a mix that retains clarity while adding excitement and intensity.

5. Creative Vocal Effects

MODERN MUSIC PRODUCTION allows for a wide range of creative effects that can completely transform your vocal sound. You can use effects like vocoders, filters, and modulation to create a unique vocal signature without needing extensive vocal skills.

Vocoder:

- Electronic Vocal Effects: A vocoder can turn your voice into an instrument, creating robotic, futuristic effects that are perfect for electronic and pop music. This effect is especially great if you're not confident in your vocal performance, as it blends your voice with synthesizer tones.

Filters:

- Lo-Fi or High-Pass Filter: Applying a high-pass filter to cut the low frequencies or a low-pass filter to remove highs can give your vocals a retro or radio-like effect. It's great for intros, outros, or breakdowns.

Modulation:

- Chorus and Flanger: Use chorus or flanger effects to add a sense of motion to your vocals, making them feel more spacey and layered. These effects work well for adding a dreamy, psychedelic quality to your sound.

6. Use Vocal Samples or Chops

IF YOU'RE NOT CONFIDENT with your raw vocals, vocal samples and chops can be an excellent way to enhance or replace your voice. Producers often use pre-recorded samples or chop up their own vocals to create new, interesting textures.

How to Use Vocal Chops:

- Chop Your Own Vocals: Take snippets of your vocal recording and rearrange them in creative ways. You can apply pitch shifting, time-stretching, and effects to create unique vocal sounds that don't require a traditional singing ability.

- Layer with Instrumentals: Place vocal chops in sync with your instrumental to create rhythmic hooks or melodic lines. This technique can add energy to your song without needing a complex vocal melody.

Sample Packs:

- Use Pre-Made Samples: Many sample libraries offer high-quality vocal samples that can fit perfectly in your production. Use these samples as part of your track, especially if you're struggling with creating a good vocal take yourself.

7. Compression for Consistent Levels

IF YOU'RE NOT A TRAINED singer, your vocal performance may lack consistency in volume. Compression is key to evening out these inconsistencies and making your vocals sound smooth and professional.

How to Use Compression:

- Control Dynamics: Compression reduces the dynamic range of your vocals, making quiet parts louder and loud parts softer. This helps your vocal sit more evenly in the mix.

- Parallel Compression: Use parallel compression to blend a heavily compressed vocal track with the original signal. This adds power and sustain to your vocals while maintaining the natural dynamics of the performance.

8. Final Tips: Focus on Emotion and Delivery

YOU DON'T HAVE TO BE a great technical singer to deliver an epic vocal performance. Focus on conveying emotion and energy in your delivery. Many of the most memorable vocal performances are not about perfection, but about how they make the listener feel.

How to Improve Your Vocal Delivery:

- Embrace Your Unique Voice: Don't try too hard to sound like someone else. Use your natural tone, and enhance it with the effects and techniques mentioned above.

- Use Emotion Over Technique: Lean into the emotion of the song. Whether it's raw energy or vulnerability, the listener will connect with authenticity, even if your vocal performance isn't technically perfect.

- Experiment with Different Styles: Try whispering, shouting, or speaking certain lines rather than singing them. Experimentation can lead to unique and captivating vocal performances.

Final Thoughts

EVEN WITHOUT FORMAL vocal training, you can create epic, professional-sounding vocals by using effects, layering, and production techniques. Whether you're subtly correcting pitch, adding space with reverb, or using distortion for intensity, the key is to experiment and find what works best for your unique sound. With modern production tools, the possibilities are endless, and your vocals can be just as epic as those of a trained singer.

Top 6 Common Guitar Recording Mistakes to Avoid for Better Sound Quality

Recording guitar can be a rewarding yet challenging process. Capturing the perfect tone and achieving professional sound quality requires attention to detail. Unfortunately, even small mistakes can make your recordings sound amateurish or lackluster. In this blog post, we'll cover six common guitar recording mistakes and how to avoid them for a cleaner, more polished sound.

1. Neglecting Proper Tuning

ONE OF THE SIMPLEST yet most overlooked mistakes is not ensuring the guitar is properly tuned before recording. Even if the tuning is slightly off, it can make the whole track sound out of key and unprofessional. Guitars can easily slip out of tune during sessions, especially when recording multiple takes.

How to Avoid It:

- Always tune your guitar before each take, and check the tuning periodically throughout the recording session.

- Use a reliable tuning pedal or app to ensure precision.

- Consider using a guitar with good tuning stability or locking tuners to avoid frequent re-tuning.

2. Choosing the Wrong Mic Placement

MICROPHONE PLACEMENT plays a crucial role in how your guitar sounds on the recording. Placing the mic too close to the sound source may result in a boomy or overly bass-heavy sound, while placing it too far can make the recording sound distant or thin. Experimenting with mic placement is essential to capturing the best tone.

How to Avoid It:

- For acoustic guitar, start by placing a condenser microphone around 12 inches away from where the neck meets the body of the guitar. Adjust the distance and angle depending on the sound you want to capture.

- For electric guitar, place the mic (usually a dynamic mic like the Shure SM57) off-center from the speaker cone to avoid harshness.

- Always monitor your sound as you adjust the placement to find the sweet spot.

3. Overloading the Gain or Input Level

RECORDING WITH THE gain set too high can lead to unwanted distortion or clipping, which causes unpleasant, distorted artifacts in your sound. On the other hand, setting the input level too low can result in weak recordings with too much background noise. Striking a balance is key.

How to Avoid It:

- Use your audio interface's input gain controls to ensure that your signal peaks between -6 dB and -3 dB. This gives you headroom without risking distortion.

- Monitor levels during the recording to ensure consistency.

- Remember, it's easier to boost a low-level signal during mixing than to fix a clipped recording.

4. Using Old or Worn-Out Strings

GUITAR STRINGS LOSE their brightness and sustain over time, making your guitar sound dull or lifeless. Recording with old strings is one of the most common mistakes that can negatively affect your tone.

How to Avoid It:

- Always change your strings before an important recording session, especially if you haven't changed them in a while.

- If you want a bright, punchy tone, opt for new strings. For a warmer sound, you can record with slightly broken-in strings (but not too old).

- Keep a backup set of strings handy during long sessions in case of breakage or wear.

5. Ignoring Background Noise

BACKGROUND NOISE CAN be a major issue, especially when recording in a home studio. Noises such as hums, air conditioning, street sounds, or even the sound of your chair creaking can be captured by sensitive microphones, compromising the quality of your guitar recording.

How to Avoid It:

- Record in a quiet, isolated space where you can control external noise.

- Use noise gates or high-pass filters to eliminate low-level hums and background noise.

- For electric guitar recordings, eliminate amp hum by using balanced cables and grounding your equipment.

6. Not Double-Tracking Guitars for Fullness

RECORDING A SINGLE guitar track often leads to a thin sound that doesn't fill out the mix. One common mistake is forgetting to double-track (recording the same part twice on separate tracks) guitars, which can add depth and fullness to your sound, especially in rock and pop music.

How to Avoid It:

- Record the same guitar part twice on separate tracks, panning each take hard left and right. This creates a fuller, wider stereo image.

- Be sure that both takes are as tight as possible for a cohesive sound.

- Experiment with slightly different tones or guitar settings for each take to add more texture and dimension.

Final Thoughts

AVOIDING THESE COMMON guitar recording mistakes can significantly improve the sound quality of your recordings. Whether you're working on an acoustic track or a full electric arrangement, proper tuning, mic placement, and attention to detail can make a world of difference. By following these tips, you'll be well on your way to capturing clean, professional-sounding guitar tracks that stand out in your mix.

Happy recording!

How to Create Ambient Pads and Atmospheres: Sound Design Techniques for Lush Soundscapes

Ambient pads and atmospheres are essential in creating expansive, lush soundscapes in music production. Whether you're producing ambient, cinematic, or even electronic genres, these elements add depth, mood, and texture to your tracks. Crafting the perfect pad or atmospheric sound requires a blend of sound design techniques, creativity, and an understanding of the tools at your disposal. In this post, we'll dive into the key techniques to create immersive pads and atmospheres for your productions.

1. Choosing the Right Synth or Sound Source

THE FOUNDATION OF ANY great pad or atmospheric sound starts with the sound source. Most digital audio workstations (DAWs) come with built-in synths, but there are also many third-party synths designed for ambient sounds. Here are a few popular options:

- Serum: A versatile wavetable synthesizer that allows for rich, evolving sounds.

- Omnisphere: Known for its extensive library of atmospheric sounds and complex textures.

- Massive X: Great for designing deep, expansive pads with intuitive controls.

- Absynth: Excellent for creating evolving pads and otherworldly textures.

While these synths are ideal, you can also experiment with recorded samples of nature, instruments, or vocal pads, then manipulate them into atmospheric sounds using effects and processing.

2. Oscillator Selection and Tuning

ONCE YOU HAVE A SYNTH, your next step is selecting the oscillators that will form the basis of your pad or atmosphere. Pads typically use multiple oscillators layered together to create a rich, thick sound. Here's how to get started:
   - Use Sine or Saw Waves: For smooth, flowing pads, start with sine waves. For a richer, brighter sound, saw waves are a good choice.
   - Detune Oscillators: Detuning one or more oscillators slightly from the fundamental pitch creates a subtle chorusing effect, adding depth and movement to the sound.
   - Layer Oscillators: Combine different waveforms (e.g., sine, saw, or triangle) or even mix in different octaves to create more complex, lush textures.

3. Applying Envelopes for Smooth Transitions

TO ACHIEVE THE CHARACTERISTIC soft attack and long release of ambient pads, it's essential to shape your sound using the amplitude envelope. This determines how the sound evolves over time.
   - Slow Attack: Increase the attack time to let the sound fade in slowly, giving it a smooth, evolving quality.
   - Long Release: Set a long release time so the pad fades out gradually after the note is released, creating a continuous and flowing soundscape.
   - Sustain and Decay: Keep the sustain level high, as pads are typically designed to hold their intensity over time without decaying too quickly.

4. Filter Movement and Modulation

FILTER MODULATION PLAYS a crucial role in adding movement to your pad or atmosphere, preventing it from sounding static or monotonous. By using filter envelopes and LFOs (Low-Frequency Oscillators), you can create evolving sounds that change subtly over time.

- Low-Pass Filter: Apply a low-pass filter to remove high frequencies and create a warmer, more atmospheric sound. Automate the filter cutoff to slowly open and close over time, adding movement.

- LFO Modulation: Assign an LFO to modulate the filter cutoff, panning, or pitch. Slow LFO rates (e.g., 0.1 to 0.3 Hz) are ideal for gradual, evolving changes that make your pad feel alive.

5. Using Reverb and Delay to Enhance Space

REVERB AND DELAY ARE your best friends when it comes to creating lush, spacious atmospheres. They help push sounds into the background, making them feel like they're floating in space.

- Reverb: Use a large hall or plate reverb to create a sense of depth and space. Experiment with the decay time and wet/dry balance to achieve the desired atmosphere. Long decay times work well for creating expansive soundscapes.

- Delay: Add a subtle delay to give the pad a sense of echo and distance. Stereo delay can also help widen the sound, making it feel more immersive. You can sync the delay to the tempo of your track for rhythmic patterns or use unsynced delays for a more organic feel.

6. Layering Sounds for Complexity

ONE OF THE BEST WAYS to achieve complex, evolving soundscapes is through layering. By combining multiple pads, textures, or sound sources, you can create a richer and more dynamic sonic experience.

- Blend Different Textures: Combine smooth, tonal pads with noisier, more textured elements to create contrast. For example, layer a lush synth pad with a field recording of wind or distant noise.

- Octave Layers: Add another layer of the same pad sound but pitched up or down an octave to increase the harmonic complexity and give your sound more depth.

7. Automation and Evolving Soundscapes

TO MAKE YOUR PADS AND atmospheres more engaging, consider automating various parameters over time. Automation allows your sound to evolve naturally and helps maintain listener interest.

- Filter Automation: Slowly automate the filter cutoff to open or close throughout the track, adding tension and release.

- Reverb and Delay Automation: Gradually increase the reverb size or delay feedback to give the sense that the pad is expanding or contracting over time.

- Volume Automation: Fade your pads in and out subtly to create swells that move with the dynamics of the song.

8. Using Granular Synthesis for Unique Textures

GRANULAR SYNTHESIS is a powerful technique for creating highly textured and evolving pads. It works by taking small "grains" of sound from a sample and manipulating them in various ways. This can lead to some truly otherworldly atmospheres.

- Start with a Sample: Load a vocal, instrument, or field recording into a granular synth, then experiment with grain size, pitch, and density to create new textures.

- Stretch and Warp: Granular synthesis excels at time-stretching, allowing you to take a short sound and stretch it out into a long, ambient pad.

Final Thoughts

CREATING AMBIENT PADS and atmospheres is both an art and a science, requiring a balance between sound design techniques and creative expression. By layering sounds, applying modulation, and using effects like reverb and delay, you can build expansive soundscapes that transport listeners into another world. Whether you're crafting music for film, ambient projects, or adding texture to electronic tracks, these techniques will help you design lush, immersive pads and atmospheres that elevate your music to the next level.

So, fire up your synths, experiment with these techniques, and let your imagination guide you in creating soundscapes that captivate and inspire.

5 Essential Things You Need to Know About Decibels (dB) for Audio Mixing and Mastering

Introduction

DECIBELS (DB) ARE A fundamental unit of measurement in audio mixing and mastering, but they can be confusing for those new to sound production. Understanding decibels is critical for managing levels, preventing distortion, and ensuring your mixes are clear, dynamic, and well-balanced. Whether you're an aspiring producer or a seasoned sound engineer, mastering the concept of decibels can make a significant difference in the quality of your audio work. In this guide, we'll break down five essential things you need to know about decibels for audio mixing and mastering.

1. What is a Decibel (dB)?

THE DECIBEL (DB) IS a logarithmic unit used to measure sound intensity, sound pressure, or voltage levels in audio. It compares the power of one sound to a reference level, which is why it's commonly used in audio mixing to express the relative loudness of signals.
 Key Facts About Decibels:
 - Logarithmic Scale: The decibel scale is logarithmic, meaning each 10 dB increase represents a tenfold increase in sound intensity. For example, 70 dB is ten times more intense than 60 dB.
 - Reference Levels: In audio, decibels can measure various things such as SPL (Sound Pressure Level) or digital levels (dBFS in digital audio). The reference point changes depending on the context.
 In practice, decibels allow sound engineers to fine-tune loudness levels and maintain consistency across different elements of a mix.

2. Understanding dBFS: Decibels Full Scale

IN DIGITAL AUDIO MIXING, the most common decibel unit is dBFS (Decibels Full Scale), which measures audio levels relative to the maximum possible signal level (0 dBFS). Anything above 0 dBFS causes clipping, resulting in distortion because the signal exceeds the maximum level that digital audio can handle.
Key Points About dBFS:
- 0 dBFS: This represents the maximum peak level in a digital system. Anything over 0 dBFS will distort.
- Negative Values: Unlike in analog systems, digital levels are always expressed as negative values when they're below 0 dBFS (e.g., -12 dBFS or -6 dBFS).

Tip: Aim to keep your master levels at around -6 dBFS to -3 dBFS when mixing to avoid clipping and allow room for mastering.

3. Signal-to-Noise Ratio (SNR) and Dynamic Range

DECIBELS ARE ALSO USED to measure the signal-to-noise ratio (SNR) and dynamic range of your audio. Both of these factors are crucial in mixing and mastering.
Signal-to-Noise Ratio:
- The SNR is the ratio between the level of your audio signal and the background noise in your recording.
- A high SNR means that the audio signal is much louder than the noise, which is desirable in professional recordings.
Dynamic Range:
- The dynamic range is the difference between the quietest and loudest parts of a signal, typically measured in decibels.
- In mixing, you want to preserve enough dynamic range so your music has depth and doesn't sound overly compressed or flat.

Tip: Aim for a balanced dynamic range in your mixes to prevent your tracks from sounding either too quiet or too "squashed."

4. How Decibels Affect Perceived Loudness

A COMMON MISCONCEPTION in audio mixing is that louder always sounds better. However, increasing the dB level indiscriminately can lead to distortion, ear fatigue, and a lack of dynamics in your music. Decibels play a crucial role in perceived loudness, which is how loud we hear something rather than its actual intensity.

Loudness and Fletcher-Munson Curve:

- The Fletcher-Munson Curve explains that our ears perceive different frequencies as louder or quieter, even at the same decibel level.

- Lower and higher frequencies are perceived as quieter at lower volumes, which is why mixing engineers often boost bass and treble at lower listening levels.

Tip: Use decibels to carefully balance loudness in different frequency ranges so that your mix translates well at various playback volumes.

5. Gain Staging and Headroom

GAIN STAGING AND HEADROOM are two critical concepts in mixing and mastering, and both involve proper use of decibels. Gain staging ensures that the signal levels are optimized throughout the recording and mixing chain without distortion.

Gain Staging:

- Involves adjusting the level of audio signals at different points in the signal chain to maintain clarity and prevent distortion.

- Start by setting your input levels properly during recording. Aim for levels between -18 dBFS and -12 dBFS in your DAW (Digital Audio Workstation).

Headroom:

- Headroom refers to the difference between your signal's peak level and 0 dBFS, which is the maximum level your digital system can handle without distortion.

- Leaving enough headroom (around -3 dBFS to -6 dBFS) ensures that mastering engineers have enough space to work with your tracks without causing distortion.

Tip: Proper gain staging prevents audio distortion and helps you create clean, professional-sounding mixes.

FAQs

1. WHAT IS THE DIFFERENCE between dBFS and dB SPL?

- dBFS refers to the decibel scale in digital audio, where 0 dBFS is the maximum level. dB SPL (Sound Pressure Level) measures the intensity of sound in the physical world, with 0 dB SPL being the threshold of human hearing.

2. Why is 0 dBFS the maximum in digital audio?

- In digital audio, 0 dBFS represents the highest level that can be recorded without clipping. Any level above this will result in digital distortion because the signal exceeds the system's capacity.

3. What is clipping and how can I avoid it?

- Clipping occurs when the audio signal exceeds 0 dBFS, causing distortion. To avoid clipping, keep your levels below 0 dBFS and leave headroom during mixing and mastering.

4. How much headroom should I leave for mastering?

- Typically, you should leave between -3 dBFS to -6 dBFS of headroom in your mix to give the mastering engineer enough space to work with.

5. Does louder music always sound better?

- Not necessarily. While louder can feel more powerful, over-compressing or boosting dB levels too much can reduce the dynamic range, causing ear fatigue and loss of clarity in your mix.

6. How do I measure decibels in my DAW?

- Most DAWs have built-in meters that measure audio levels in decibels (dBFS). Watch these meters to ensure that your signal levels stay in the safe range (below 0 dBFS).

BY MASTERING THESE essential concepts of decibels in audio mixing and mastering, you'll have a clearer understanding of how to manage your audio levels effectively. With the right balance, you can create dynamic, high-quality mixes that sound professional across various playback systems.

How to Use Audio Panning: Techniques to Enhance Song Quality in Music Production

Introduction to Audio Panning

AUDIO PANNING IS A fundamental concept in music production that involves placing audio signals within the stereo field. It allows you to position sounds left, right, or center, helping to create spatial dynamics that enhance the overall quality of a song. Panning is crucial in defining how listeners experience the music, making it an essential tool for music producers.

In this guide, we'll explore various techniques on how to use audio panning effectively, from the basics to advanced methods, ensuring your productions sound dynamic and professional.

History of Audio Panning

THE CONCEPT OF AUDIO panning traces back to the development of stereo sound in the early 20th century. Early applications in classical music involved placing orchestral sections across the stereo field to mimic the natural spatial arrangement in concert halls. As technology advanced, panning became a staple in modern music genres, allowing producers to achieve more immersive and balanced mixes.

Basic Concepts of Audio Panning

TO UNDERSTAND AUDIO panning, it's crucial to differentiate between mono and stereo sound. Mono represents a single audio channel, while stereo utilizes two, giving the illusion of space and depth. The pan knob is a key tool in controlling where an audio signal is placed within the stereo field, whether it's pushed to the left, right, or kept in the center.

Benefits of Audio Panning in Music

ONE OF THE MAIN BENEFITS of panning is that it enhances spatial perception. By spreading instruments and vocals across the stereo field, you create space for each element to breathe, reducing the likelihood of muddiness in the mix. It also allows for the creation of a more dynamic listening experience, adding depth and dimension.

Tools for Audio Panning

MOST DIGITAL AUDIO Workstations (DAWs) offer robust panning features. Popular DAWs like Ableton Live, Logic Pro, and Pro Tools provide intuitive controls that let you pan individual tracks with ease. Additionally, external hardware and plugins such as auto-panners can add a creative flair by automatically moving sounds across the stereo field.

Panning Techniques for Instruments

WHEN MIXING DRUMS, you can use panning to replicate the natural layout of a drum kit. For example, the kick and snare typically stay centered, while cymbals and toms can be panned slightly left or right. Guitars and synths, when panned effectively, can help widen the mix, providing balance and energy to the overall sound.

Vocal Panning Techniques

IN MOST CASES, LEAD vocals are kept centered in the mix for clarity and focus. However, harmonies and background vocals can be panned to the sides to create a fuller sound. Using subtle panning on vocal doubles can enhance depth without drawing attention away from the lead.

Creative Panning Techniques

EXPERIMENTATION IS key to unlocking the full potential of panning. Auto-panning effects, which move sounds across the stereo field over time, can add movement and excitement to a track. Similarly, panning automation allows you to change the position of sounds dynamically throughout the song, keeping the listener engaged.

Common Mistakes in Panning

ONE COMMON MISTAKE is over-panning, where instruments are pushed too far to the edges of the stereo field, making the mix sound unbalanced. Another is failing to achieve a cohesive stereo image, where elements feel disjointed or disconnected. Striking a balance is crucial for a polished mix.

Advanced Audio Panning Techniques

FOR MORE EXPERIENCED producers, LCR panning (Left, Center, Right) is an advanced technique that places elements strictly in these three positions. This method provides a distinct sense of space while maintaining clarity. Another approach is frequency-based panning, where lower frequencies remain centered, and higher frequencies are spread across the stereo field.

Panning for Different Genres

PANNING PREFERENCES often vary by genre. In rock and pop production, guitars and drums are frequently panned wide to create a lively mix. In electronic music, panning is used creatively to achieve unique spatial effects, while in classical and jazz, more natural panning is employed to reflect real-world performance spaces.

Surround Sound and 3D Panning

WITH THE RISE OF SURROUND sound and 3D audio, panning has evolved beyond stereo. Producers can now place sounds in a full 360-degree space, providing an even more immersive experience for the listener. These techniques are commonly used in film and virtual reality sound design but are also making their way into music production.

The Role of Panning in Live Sound

PANNING IN A LIVE SETTING presents unique challenges compared to studio production. Live engineers must consider the physical environment and audience location when deciding how to pan instruments and vocals. Achieving a balanced stereo image in a live setting requires careful planning and execution.

Mastering with Panning Considerations

DURING THE MASTERING phase, producers must ensure that the stereo width of the track translates well across different playback systems, from headphones to car speakers. Overly wide panning can cause issues in mono playback, so it's essential to keep this in mind.

Final Thoughts on Panning

EFFECTIVE PANNING CAN significantly enhance the emotional impact of a song by creating space and depth within the mix. With practice, you'll develop a keen ear for how to use panning creatively and professionally, taking your music production to the next level.

FAQs

1. HOW DO I KNOW IF I've panned too much?

- If your mix sounds unbalanced, or certain instruments feel isolated, you may have over-panned. A good rule of thumb is to ensure there's a sense of cohesion between all elements.

2. What tools should beginners use for audio panning?

- Start with the built-in panning controls in your DAW. Plugins like Soundtoys PanMan or Waves S1 Stereo Imager are also excellent for creative panning.

3. How does panning affect the mixing of vocals and instruments?

- Panning helps separate vocals and instruments, reducing muddiness and allowing

each element to be heard clearly.

4. Are there any genre-specific panning rules?

- While every genre has its norms, panning is ultimately subjective. Experiment to find what works best for your song's style and vibe.

5. How can I get better at using panning creatively?

- Listen to professionally mixed tracks in your genre and pay attention to how panning is used. Experiment with different panning techniques in your own productions to see what works best.

6. Does panning affect mastering, and how?

- Yes, panning decisions in the mix can impact how well your track translates in different listening environments. Overly wide panning can result in issues during mono playback.

Music Website Security: Protecting Against Hacks and Attacks

In today's digital age, a music website is not just a platform to showcase your talent—it's an essential part of your brand and a key tool for connecting with fans, selling merchandise, and promoting gigs. However, with the increasing prevalence of cyber threats, ensuring your website's security is crucial. A breach can result in loss of sensitive data, downtime, and damage to your reputation. This blog post explores the importance of music website security and provides practical steps to protect your site from hacks and attacks.

Why Website Security Matters for Musicians

FOR MUSICIANS, A WEBSITE is often the hub of all online activities. It's where fans go to learn about your latest releases, buy tickets, and purchase merchandise. A secure website ensures that your visitors can interact with your site without risk, protects your data, and maintains the trust you've built with your audience.

1. Protecting Sensitive Data:

Your website likely collects sensitive information, such as email addresses, payment details, and personal information from fans. A security breach could lead to this data being compromised, resulting in financial loss and legal consequences.

2. Preserving Your Reputation:

A hacked website can lead to defacement, unauthorized content, or even the spread of malware. Such incidents can damage your reputation, alienate fans, and erode trust in your brand.

3. Ensuring Continuous Operation:

A cyberattack can bring your website down, making it inaccessible to fans and disrupting your online activities. Downtime can lead to lost revenue and missed opportunities, especially if the breach occurs during a major release or tour announcement.

Common Threats to Music Websites

UNDERSTANDING THE COMMON threats that music websites face is the first step in defending against them. Here are some of the most prevalent cyber threats:

1. Malware and Ransomware:

Malware is malicious software designed to damage or gain unauthorized access to your website. Ransomware is a specific type of malware that locks your data or website until a ransom is paid. These attacks can lead to significant downtime and data loss.

2. Brute Force Attacks:

In brute force attacks, hackers use automated tools to try numerous combinations of usernames and passwords until they gain access to your site. Weak passwords or using default login credentials can make your site particularly vulnerable.

3. DDoS Attacks:

Distributed Denial of Service (DDoS) attacks flood your website with excessive traffic, overwhelming your server and causing your site to crash. This type of attack can render your website inaccessible for extended periods.

4. SQL Injection:

SQL injection attacks involve inserting malicious code into your website's database through vulnerable input fields, such as contact forms or search boxes. This can allow hackers to access, modify, or delete data stored on your site.

5. Phishing and Social Engineering:

Phishing involves tricking users into revealing sensitive information by disguising as a trustworthy entity. Social engineering attacks exploit human psychology to gain access to confidential information. Both can lead to unauthorized access to your website.

Essential Steps to Secure Your Music Website

NOW THAT YOU'RE AWARE of the threats, let's explore practical steps you can take to secure your music website and protect it from hacks and attacks.

1. Choose a Secure Hosting Provider

Your hosting provider plays a crucial role in your website's security. Choose a reputable provider that offers strong security features, including regular backups, firewalls, and DDoS protection. Ensure they provide SSL (Secure Socket Layer) certificates, which encrypt data transmitted between your website and visitors, protecting sensitive information.

2. Keep Your Software Updated

Outdated software is one of the most common vulnerabilities exploited by hackers. Regularly update your content management system (CMS), plugins, themes, and any other software your website relies on. These updates often include security patches that address known vulnerabilities.

3. Use Strong, Unique Passwords

Weak passwords are a significant security risk. Ensure that all user accounts associated with your website use strong, unique passwords that include a mix of letters, numbers, and special characters. Avoid using easily guessable passwords, and consider using a password manager to keep track of your credentials.

4. Enable Two-Factor Authentication (2FA)

Two-factor authentication adds an extra layer of security by requiring a second form of verification in addition to your password.

This could be a code sent to your mobile device or an authentication app. Enabling 2FA can significantly reduce the risk of unauthorized access to your site.

5. Regularly Back Up Your Website

Regular backups are essential to recovering your website in the event of a cyberattack. Set up automated backups with your hosting provider, and store copies in multiple locations, such as cloud storage and external drives. This ensures you can restore your site quickly if needed.

6. Implement a Web Application Firewall (WAF)

A Web Application Firewall (WAF) acts as a barrier between your website and the internet, filtering out malicious traffic before it reaches your site. WAFs can protect against a wide range of threats, including SQL injections, cross-site scripting, and brute force attacks.

7. Monitor Your Website for Suspicious Activity

Regularly monitoring your website for unusual activity can help you identify potential threats before they escalate. Use security plugins or third-party services that provide real-time monitoring, alerts, and detailed logs of all activities on your site.

8. Secure Your Login Page

Your website's login page is a common target for hackers. Secure it by limiting login attempts to prevent brute force attacks, hiding the default login URL, and using Captcha to verify users. Additionally, consider restricting access to the login page by IP address, so only trusted devices can log in.

9. Educate Your Team

If you work with a team, ensure that everyone is aware of basic security practices, such as recognizing phishing attempts, using strong passwords, and keeping software updated. The more knowledgeable your team is, the better equipped you'll be to prevent security breaches.

Conclusion

IN THE DIGITAL AGE, securing your music website is not optional—it's a necessity. By understanding the threats and implementing these essential security measures, you can protect your site against hacks and attacks, ensuring it remains a safe and reliable platform for your fans. Remember, a secure website not only safeguards your data but also preserves the trust and confidence your audience has in your brand. Taking the time to secure your site today can save you from potential headaches and losses in the future.

Creating Engaging Visual Content: Design Tips

In today's digital landscape, visual content is king. Whether it's a social media post, album cover, or promotional flyer, eye-catching visuals can captivate your audience and elevate your brand. However, creating engaging visual content requires more than just slapping a few images together. It's about thoughtful design, consistency, and creativity. Here are some essential design tips to help you with visual content design tips that resonate with your audience and enhance your online presence.

1. Understand Your Brand Identity

Before you start designing, it's crucial to have a clear understanding of your brand identity. What are the key messages and emotions you want to convey? What colors, fonts, and imagery best represent your brand? Establishing a consistent visual identity will make your content instantly recognizable and reinforce your brand's message.

For instance, if your music has a laid-back, beachy vibe, you might use soft blues, sandy tones, and relaxed typography in your visuals.

2. Keep It Simple

One of the most common design mistakes is overcomplicating visuals with too many elements. Simplicity is key to creating content that's easy to digest and visually appealing. Focus on a single, strong visual message, and avoid cluttering your design with unnecessary text, images, or graphics. Clean, minimalistic designs often have the most impact and are easier for your audience to engage with.

3. Use High-Quality Images

The quality of your images can make or break your visual content. Always use high-resolution images to ensure your designs look professional and polished. Blurry or pixelated images can detract from your message and make your content appear unprofessional. If you're taking your own photos, pay attention to lighting, composition, and focus to capture the best shots.

4. Leverage Color Psychology

Colors have a powerful impact on emotions and can significantly influence how your audience perceives your content. Understanding color psychology can help you choose the right color palette to evoke the desired response. For example, red is often associated with energy and passion, while blue can convey calmness and trust. Use color strategically to enhance the mood and message of your visual content.

5. Prioritize Readability

If your visual content includes text, readability should be a top priority. Choose fonts that are easy to read and avoid overly decorative or complex typefaces. Ensure there's enough contrast between your text and background so that the words stand out clearly. Additionally, limit the number of fonts you use in a single design to maintain a cohesive and professional look.

Pro Tip: Stick to one or two fonts that complement each other—one for headlines and another for body text.

6. Use the Rule of Thirds

The rule of thirds is a fundamental design principle that can help you create balanced and visually appealing compositions. Imagine your design divided into a 3x3 grid. Place key elements along these grid lines or at their intersections to create a more dynamic and engaging layout. This technique is particularly useful for photography and social media posts.

7. Incorporate White Space

White space, or negative space, is the empty area around your design elements. While it might be tempting to fill every inch of your design, white space is crucial for creating a clean and uncluttered look. It helps direct the viewer's attention to the most important parts of your design and prevents your content from feeling overwhelming.

8. Be Consistent Across Platforms

Consistency is key to building a strong visual brand. Ensure that your visual content is consistent across all platforms, from social media and your website to promotional materials. This means using the same color schemes, fonts, and design elements to create a cohesive look and feel. Consistency helps reinforce your brand identity and makes your content more recognizable to your audience.

9. Tell a Story with Your Visuals

Great visuals do more than just look good—they tell a story. Whether it's a behind-the-scenes glimpse of your creative process, a visual representation of your lyrics, or a photo that captures the essence of your music, your visuals should convey a narrative that resonates with your audience. Think about the story you want to tell with each piece of visual content and design with that narrative in mind.

10. Test and Iterate

Design is an iterative process. Don't be afraid to test different visual styles and layouts to see what resonates best with your audience. Pay attention to the engagement metrics on your posts—likes, shares, comments, and clicks can all provide valuable insights into what works and what doesn't. Use this feedback to refine your designs and continually improve your visual content strategy.

Conclusion

CREATING ENGAGING VISUAL content is a powerful way to connect with your audience and strengthen your brand. By understanding your brand identity, keeping your designs simple, leveraging color psychology, and prioritizing readability, you can craft visuals that not only look great but also resonate with your fans. Remember, consistency, storytelling, and iteration are key to mastering the art of visual content. With these design tips in mind, you'll be well on your way to creating visuals that captivate and inspire.

Podcasting for Musicians: Troubleshooting Audio Recording

In the ever-evolving world of music, podcasting has emerged as a powerful tool for musicians to connect with fans, share their insights, and showcase their creativity. Starting your own podcast can be an exciting venture, but it also comes with its own set of challenges, particularly when it comes to audio recording. Poor audio quality can detract from your content and frustrate listeners, making troubleshooting a crucial skill for any podcaster. In this blog post *"Podcasting for Musicians: Troubleshooting Audio Recording"*, we'll dive into the common audio recording issues musicians face when starting a podcast and provide practical tips for troubleshooting and achieving high-quality sound.

Why Audio Quality Matters

THE IMPACT OF AUDIO Quality on Listener Experience

Audio quality is paramount in podcasting because it directly affects the listener's experience. Clear, crisp sound makes it easier for your audience to engage with your content and stay focused on your message. Poor audio quality, on the other hand, can be distracting and lead to listener frustration, causing them to tune out or abandon your podcast altogether.

The Professionalism Factor

High-quality audio reflects professionalism and shows that you take your podcast seriously. It enhances your credibility and helps you build a strong reputation in the podcasting community. Investing time and effort into achieving excellent sound quality is an investment in your podcast's success.

Common Audio Recording Issues and How to Troubleshoot Them

1. BACKGROUND NOISE

Problem: Background noise, such as hums, hisses, or ambient sounds, can interfere with your recording and make it difficult for listeners to hear your content clearly.

Solution: Use a quality microphone with good noise-canceling capabilities, and ensure your recording environment is as quiet as possible. Consider using soundproofing materials or recording in a space with minimal echo. Additionally, software tools like noise gates and noise reduction plugins can help clean up audio in post-production.

2. Poor Microphone Placement

Problem: Incorrect microphone placement can result in uneven sound quality, with some parts of your recording being too loud or too soft.

Solution: Position your microphone at an optimal distance from your mouth, usually about 6-12 inches. Use a pop filter to reduce plosive sounds and a shock mount to minimize vibrations. Experiment with different placements to find the best position for clear and consistent sound.

3. Distorted Audio

Problem: Audio distortion occurs when the recording level is too high, causing clipping and a distorted sound.

Solution: Adjust your microphone's gain settings to ensure you're not recording at a level that exceeds the maximum capacity. Monitor your audio levels using headphones during recording and keep the levels within the recommended range. Most recording software has visual indicators to help you manage levels effectively.

4. Echo and Reverberation

Problem: Echo and reverberation can make your audio sound hollow or distant, affecting clarity.

Solution: To reduce echo, record in a room with soft furnishings or use sound-absorbing materials like acoustic panels. Avoid recording in large, empty spaces that amplify sound reflections. If you encounter echo in post-production, use software tools to reduce reverb.

5. Audio Sync Issues

Problem: Audio sync issues occur when your audio and video (if applicable) are out of alignment, leading to awkward or confusing content.

Solution: Ensure your recording setup is properly synchronized. Check your software settings to confirm that your audio and video are captured at the same frame rate and sample rate. Use editing software to align audio and video tracks if necessary.

6. Inconsistent Volume Levels

Problem: Inconsistent volume levels can result in an uneven listening experience, with some parts of your podcast being too loud or too soft.

Solution: Use a compressor to even out volume levels and ensure consistency throughout your podcast. You can also normalize audio levels during post-production to achieve a balanced sound. Regularly check and adjust levels as needed during recording.

Choosing the Right Equipment

MICROPHONES

Investing in a high-quality microphone is one of the best ways to ensure clear and professional-sounding audio. Dynamic microphones are often recommended for podcasting due to their ability to reject background noise, while condenser microphones offer a broader frequency response for studio-quality sound.

Audio Interfaces

An audio interface connects your microphone to your computer and converts analog sound into digital audio. Choose an interface with good preamps and low latency to ensure high-quality recordings. Some popular options include Focusrite Scarlett and PreSonus AudioBox.

Headphones

High-quality headphones are essential for monitoring your audio during recording and editing. Look for closed-back headphones that offer good sound isolation and accurate sound reproduction. Brands like Audio-Technica and Beyerdynamic are known for their reliable podcasting headphones.

Recording Software

Choosing the right recording software is crucial for capturing and editing your podcast audio. Popular options include Adobe Audition, Audacity (free), and GarageBand (for Mac users). Familiarize yourself with the features and settings of your chosen software to make the most of your recordings.

Editing and Post-Production

CLEANING UP YOUR AUDIO

Editing is where you refine your podcast audio and remove any unwanted noise or mistakes. Use audio editing software to cut out sections, adjust levels, and apply noise reduction. Pay attention to details like breath sounds and background noise to ensure a polished final product.

Adding Music and Effects

Incorporating music and sound effects can enhance your podcast and make it more engaging. However, ensure that these elements are used sparingly and do not overshadow your spoken content. Use royalty-free music or obtain the necessary licenses for any music you include.

Finalizing Your Podcast

Once your audio is edited and polished, listen to the entire podcast to ensure it meets your quality standards. Check for any remaining issues, such as inconsistent levels or abrupt transitions, and make final adjustments as needed. Export your podcast in a suitable format (e.g., MP3) for distribution.

Conclusion

PODCASTING OFFERS MUSICIANS a fantastic platform to share their stories, insights, and creativity with a wider audience. However, achieving high-quality audio recording is essential for creating a professional and enjoyable listening experience. By troubleshooting common audio issues, choosing the right equipment, and investing time in editing, you can ensure that your podcast stands out and resonates with your audience. Remember, practice and patience are key to mastering the art of podcasting. With these strategies, you'll be well on your way to creating a successful podcast that showcases your talent and connects with your listeners.

FAQs

FAQ 1: WHAT TYPE OF microphone is best for podcasting?

Dynamic microphones are often preferred for podcasting due to their ability to reject background noise and focus on the speaker's voice. However, condenser microphones can also be used for studio-quality sound.

FAQ 2: How can I reduce background noise in my recordings?

To reduce background noise, use a quality microphone with noise-canceling features, record in a quiet environment, and use soundproofing materials. Software tools like noise reduction plugins can also help clean up audio in post-production.

FAQ 3: What should I do if my audio is distorted?

If your audio is distorted, check and adjust your microphone's gain settings to avoid clipping. Monitor audio levels during recording and keep them within the recommended range to prevent distortion.

FAQ 4: How can I fix echo in my recordings?

To fix echo, record in a room with soft furnishings or use sound-absorbing materials like acoustic panels. If echo persists, use software tools to reduce reverb during post-production.

FAQ 5: What equipment do I need to start a podcast?

To start a podcast, you'll need a high-quality microphone, an audio interface, closed-back headphones, and recording software. Investing in good equipment will help ensure professional-sounding audio for your podcast.

How To Make Your Guitar Strings Last Longer: A Guide for Musicians

Guitar strings are an essential component of your instrument, directly influencing your sound and playing experience. However, they can wear out quickly if not properly cared for, leading to dull tones, increased breakage, and more frequent replacements. If you're looking to make your guitar strings last longer, follow these practical tips to keep them in top condition for longer.

1. Wash Your Hands Before Playing

One of the simplest yet most effective ways to prolong the life of your guitar strings is to wash your hands before playing. Natural oils, dirt, and sweat from your hands can accumulate on the strings, causing them to corrode faster. Clean hands reduce the amount of grime that comes into contact with your strings, helping to keep them fresher for longer.

2. Wipe Down Your Strings After Each Use

After playing, it's important to wipe down your strings with a clean, dry cloth. This removes any sweat, dirt, or oils that may have transferred from your fingers during your session. By taking a few moments to do this after each practice or performance, you can significantly slow down the process of string degradation.

3. Use String Cleaners and Lubricants

There are products specifically designed to clean and lubricate guitar strings. These cleaners help to remove grime and protect the strings from rust and corrosion. Lubricants can also reduce friction, making the strings feel smoother and easier to play while extending their lifespan. Apply these products according to the manufacturer's instructions for the best results.

4. Store Your Guitar Properly

Proper storage of your guitar can also contribute to the longevity of your strings. Keep your guitar in a case when not in use to protect it from dust, moisture, and temperature fluctuations, all of which can affect string quality. If you live in a particularly humid or dry climate, consider using a humidity control system in your guitar case to maintain an optimal environment.

5. Change Your Strings Regularly

While the goal is to make your strings last as long as possible, they won't last forever. Changing your strings regularly before they reach the point of breaking or sounding dull can actually save you money in the long run. This is because old strings can put more stress on your guitar's neck and hardware, leading to costly repairs.

6. Play With Clean Technique

How you play can also impact the lifespan of your strings. If you tend to have a heavy touch or frequently bend strings, they may wear out faster. Developing a clean technique with a lighter touch can reduce the strain on your strings, helping them last longer. Additionally, consider using coated strings, which are designed to be more durable and resist corrosion.

7. Consider the Right String Material

Different string materials have varying lifespans. For example, coated strings generally last longer than uncoated ones because they have a protective layer that resists corrosion. Stainless steel strings are also known for their durability. When choosing strings, consider your playing style and how often you perform to select a material that meets your needs for longevity.

Final Thoughts

EXTENDING THE LIFE of your guitar strings is not only about saving money but also about maintaining the quality of your sound and the playability of your instrument. By incorporating these habits into your routine, you can keep your strings in excellent

condition for longer, allowing you to focus on what matters most—making music.

Remember, a little care goes a long way in preserving the vitality of your strings, so take the time to maintain them properly and enjoy a better playing experience.

Best Microphone Placement Tips for Optimal Sound

Proper microphone placement is crucial to capturing high-quality audio, whether you're recording in a studio, performing live, or giving a speech. The placement of your microphone can significantly impact the clarity, warmth, and overall sound of your voice or instrument. Below are some essential tips for best microphone placement tips to achieve the best possible results.

1. Understand the Microphone Type

- Dynamic Microphones: These are great for live performances because they're durable and less sensitive to background noise. Place them close to the sound source.

- Condenser Microphones: These are more sensitive and better for studio recordings. They can capture more detail but require careful placement to avoid picking up unwanted noise.

- Ribbon Microphones: Known for their warm, natural sound, these are typically used in studio settings. They are delicate, so handle and place them with care.

2. Distance from the Sound Source

- Vocals: Place the microphone 6-12 inches from the vocalist's mouth. Closer placement increases bass response (the proximity effect), which can add warmth but might need balancing with EQ.

- Instruments: For string instruments, place the microphone about 6 inches away, aiming it at where the sound resonates most (e.g., the sound hole of a guitar). For brass and woodwinds, place the microphone about 1-2 feet away from the bell or sound source.

3. Angle and Position

- Vocals: Angle the microphone slightly off-axis (not directly in front of the mouth) to reduce plosive sounds (like "p" and "b" sounds). This also helps in reducing sibilance (harsh "s" sounds).

- Acoustic Guitar: Position the microphone near the 12th fret, about 6 inches away, and angle it slightly toward the sound hole for a balanced tone.

- Drums: For the snare drum, place the microphone just above the rim, angled towards the center. For the kick drum, position the microphone inside the drum, near the beater, or outside, just in front of the resonant head, depending on the desired sound.

4. Avoiding Reflections and Feedback

- Live Performances: Keep microphones away from speakers and monitor wedges to prevent feedback. Angle the microphone away from reflective surfaces like walls or hard floors to reduce unwanted echoes.

- Studio Settings: Use acoustic treatments like foam panels or bass traps around the microphone to reduce reflections and improve the clarity of the recording.

5. Use Pop Filters and Windscreens

- Pop Filters: Place a pop filter 2-4 inches in front of the microphone when recording vocals. This reduces plosive sounds and helps maintain a consistent distance between the singer and the microphone.

- Windscreens: For outdoor recordings, use a windscreen to reduce wind noise. Position it securely over the microphone, ensuring it doesn't touch the microphone diaphragm.

6. Experiment with Placement

- Sweet Spot: Every room and every sound source is different. Don't be afraid to experiment with microphone placement to find the "sweet spot" where the sound is most balanced and clear.

- Room Sound: Consider how much of the room's natural reverb you want in the recording. Moving the microphone closer to the sound source reduces room noise, while placing it further away can capture more of the room's ambiance.

7. Monitor Your Sound

- Headphones: Always monitor your sound with high-quality headphones during setup. This allows you to hear any issues in real-time and adjust the microphone placement accordingly.

- Sound Check: Perform a thorough sound check before recording or going live. Walk around the space with your microphone to identify any problem areas, and adjust the placement as needed.

Conclusion

THE WAY YOU PLACE YOUR microphone can make a significant difference in the quality of your sound. By understanding the type of microphone you're using, considering distance and angle, and taking the environment into account, you can optimize your microphone placement for any situation. Whether you're aiming for crisp, clear vocals or a rich, full instrument sound, these tips will help you capture the best possible audio.

Mastering Music Production in FL Studio

In the realm of music production, creativity knows no bounds. For those aspiring to craft melodies that resonate with listeners on a profound level, mastering FL Studio is paramount. This comprehensive software offers a treasure trove of tools and features that can elevate your music to new heights. If you're ready to embark on a journey of sonic exploration, read on as we delve into a step-by-step guide on how to master music production with FL Studio.

Step 1: Familiarize Yourself with FL Studio

Before diving headfirst into the world of music production, take the time to familiarize yourself with the FL Studio interface. Explore its various functions, tools, and menus to gain a solid understanding of how the software operates. By mastering the basics, you'll set a strong foundation for your music production journey.

Step 2: Learn the Fundamentals of Music Theory

While FL Studio provides a myriad of capabilities, a solid understanding of music theory is essential for crafting harmonious compositions. Brush up on the basics of melody, harmony, rhythm, and song structure to enhance your compositions and arrangements. Remember, music production is as much about artistry as it is about technical prowess.

Step 3: Experiment with Different Genres and Styles

One of the beauties of FL Studio is its versatility. Experiment with different genres and musical styles to find your unique sound. Whether you're drawn to the rhythmic beats of hip-hop or the ethereal melodies of electronic music, let your creativity roam free. Embrace the opportunity to blend genres and create music that is uniquely yours.

Step 4: Dive into Sound Design and Sampling

Sound design is a crucial aspect of music production that can elevate your tracks to a professional level. Explore FL Studio's vast array of synthesizers, effects, and sampling tools to sculpt your sound. Experiment with layering sounds, manipulating audio samples, and creating custom presets to craft a signature sound that sets your music apart.

Step 5: Master the Art of Mixing and Mastering

A polished mix can make all the difference in the impact of your music. Dive into the intricacies of mixing and mastering to ensure that every element of your track shines. Experiment with EQ, compression, reverb, and other effects to achieve a balanced and dynamic mix that captivates listeners.

Step 6: Embrace Collaboration and Feedback

Music production is a collaborative art form. Seek out opportunities to collaborate with other artists, share your work, and receive feedback. Embracing collaboration can introduce fresh perspectives and ideas that push your creativity to new heights. Don't be afraid to share your creations with the world and grow as an artist.

Step 7: Practice, Patience, and Perseverance

Lastly, mastering music production with FL Studio requires practice, patience, and perseverance. Rome wasn't built in a day, and neither will your music career. Dedicate time to honing your craft, experimenting with new techniques, and pushing the boundaries of your creativity. Remember, the journey to mastery is a marathon, not a sprint.

AS YOU EMBARK ON YOUR music production journey with FL Studio, keep in mind that creativity is your greatest asset. Let your passion for music drive you forward, and don't be afraid to explore the depths of your imagination. With dedication and perseverance, you'll unlock a world of sonic possibilities that await at your fingertips.

So, what are you waiting for? Dive into the realm of music production with FL Studio and unleash your creativity like never before. The world is waiting to hear the melodies that only you can create.

Website Accessibility: Ensuring Inclusivity for All Fans

Introduction

IN TODAY'S DIGITAL age, your website is often the first point of contact between you and your audience. Whether you're a musician, a brand, or a content creator, having an accessible website is crucial. But what does it mean for a website to be accessible? Simply put, it's about ensuring that all users, regardless of their abilities or disabilities, can navigate and interact with your site effectively. In this blog post, we'll explore the importance of website accessibility, discuss common barriers that users face, and provide practical tips to make your site inclusive for all fans.

Why Website Accessibility Matters

REACHING A WIDER AUDIENCE

Accessibility isn't just about doing the right thing; it's also about expanding your reach. According to the World Health Organization, over 1 billion people worldwide live with some form of disability. This means that if your website isn't accessible, you could be alienating a significant portion of your potential audience. By making your site accessible, you ensure that everyone, including those with disabilities, can enjoy your content and connect with you.

Legal and Ethical Considerations

Beyond the moral imperative, there are legal reasons to prioritize accessibility. Many countries have laws and regulations that require websites to be accessible to people with disabilities. In the United States, for example, the Americans with Disabilities Act (ADA) has been interpreted to include websites under its accessibility requirements. Failing to comply with these laws can result in legal action, as well as damage to your reputation.

Enhancing User Experience

Website accessibility also enhances the overall user experience. When a site is easy to navigate and use for everyone, it creates a more enjoyable experience for all visitors. Accessible design often leads to a cleaner, more intuitive interface, benefiting users both with and without disabilities.

Common Accessibility Barriers

VISUAL IMPAIRMENTS

One of the most common barriers is related to visual impairments. Users who are blind or have low vision may rely on screen readers to navigate websites. If your site isn't compatible with screen readers, these users could miss out on crucial information.

Hearing Impairments

For users with hearing impairments, audio content without captions or transcripts can be a significant barrier. Whether it's a podcast, video, or music clip, ensuring that all audio content is accompanied by text alternatives is essential.

Motor Disabilities

Users with motor disabilities may have difficulty using a mouse or other pointing devices. If your website relies heavily on mouse-based navigation, it could be challenging for these users to interact with your content. Ensuring keyboard accessibility is key to overcoming this barrier.

Cognitive and Learning Disabilities

Cognitive and learning disabilities can make it difficult for some users to process complex information or navigate complicated layouts. Websites that are cluttered or confusing can be particularly challenging for these users. Simplifying your design and content can help make your site more accessible to everyone.

Steps to Make Your Website Accessible

STEP 1: USE SEMANTIC HTML

Semantic HTML refers to using HTML elements that clearly describe their meaning and purpose. For example, using `<header>`, `<nav>`, and `<footer>` tags instead of generic `<div>` tags helps screen readers and other assistive technologies understand the structure of your site. This makes it easier for users with disabilities to navigate your content.

Step 2: Ensure Keyboard Accessibility

Make sure that all interactive elements on your site, such as links, buttons, and forms, can be accessed and used via keyboard. This is crucial for users with motor disabilities who may not be able to use a mouse. Test your site by navigating it using only the keyboard to ensure that all functionality is accessible.

Step 3: Provide Text Alternatives for Non-Text Content

For any non-text content, such as images, videos, and audio, provide text alternatives. This could include alt text for images, captions for videos, and transcripts for audio files. These text alternatives allow screen readers to convey the content to users with visual or hearing impairments.

Step 4: Use ARIA Landmarks and Roles

ARIA (Accessible Rich Internet Applications) landmarks and roles are attributes that can be added to HTML elements to improve accessibility. These attributes help screen readers understand the purpose of different sections and elements on your page, making navigation easier for users with disabilities.

Step 5: Optimize for Screen Readers

Screen readers are essential tools for users with visual impairments. To optimize your site for screen readers, ensure that your content is properly structured with headings, lists, and paragraphs. Avoid using images of text, as these are often unreadable by screen readers.

Step 6: Design with Contrast and Color in Mind

Color contrast is important for users with visual impairments, including color blindness. Make sure that your text has sufficient contrast with the background to be easily readable. Tools like the Web Content Accessibility Guidelines (WCAG) contrast checker can help you determine if your color choices meet accessibility standards.

Step 7: Simplify Navigation and Layout

A simple, intuitive layout benefits all users, especially those with cognitive or learning disabilities. Avoid clutter and ensure that your navigation is straightforward. Use clear, descriptive labels for links and buttons, and consider adding a search function to help users find what they're looking for quickly.

Step 8: Test Your Website's Accessibility

Once you've implemented these steps, it's important to test your website's accessibility. There are several tools available, such as WAVE and Axe, that can help you identify accessibility issues. Additionally, consider conducting user testing with individuals who have disabilities to get firsthand feedback on your site's accessibility.

Benefits of an Accessible Website

IMPROVED SEO

Accessibility and search engine optimization (SEO) go hand in hand. Many accessibility best practices, such as using alt text for images and creating a clear site structure, also benefit SEO. By making your site accessible, you can improve its search engine rankings, leading to increased visibility and traffic.

Better Engagement and Retention

An accessible website leads to better engagement and retention rates. When all users can easily navigate and interact with your content, they're more likely to stay on your site longer, return in the future, and recommend it to others. This can help build a loyal fan base and increase your reach.

Positive Brand Image

By prioritizing accessibility, you demonstrate a commitment to inclusivity and social responsibility. This can enhance your brand's reputation and help you connect with a broader audience. Fans and customers are more likely to support brands that align with their values, and accessibility is a key aspect of this.

Conclusion

ENSURING THAT YOUR website is accessible is not just a technical task; it's a commitment to inclusivity and respect for all users. By taking the time to identify and remove accessibility barriers, you can create a website that welcomes everyone, regardless of their abilities. This not only broadens your reach but also enhances your brand's reputation and user experience. Start today by implementing the steps outlined in this guide, and make your site a place where all fans can connect and engage.

FAQs

FAQ 1: WHAT IS WEBSITE accessibility?

Website accessibility refers to the practice of making websites usable for all people, including those with disabilities, by removing barriers that might prevent them from interacting with or navigating the site.

FAQ 2: Why is accessibility important for my website?

Accessibility is important because it ensures that everyone, regardless of their abilities, can access and use your website. This expands your audience, improves user experience, and helps you comply with legal requirements.

FAQ 3: How can I test my website for accessibility?

You can test your website for accessibility using tools like WAVE, Axe, or the WCAG contrast checker. Additionally, user testing with individuals who have disabilities can provide valuable insights.

FAQ 4: What are some common accessibility issues on websites?

Common accessibility issues include lack of alt text for images, poor color contrast, non-keyboard accessible navigation, and lack of text alternatives for audio and video content.

FAQ 5: Can improving accessibility benefit my website's SEO?

Yes, many accessibility best practices also benefit SEO. For example, using alt text for images and ensuring a clear site structure can improve your site's search engine rankings.

Tour Planning: Overcoming Logistics and Scheduling Hurdles

Introduction

PLANNING A TOUR IS an exciting yet daunting task. Whether you're a musician hitting the road for the first time or a seasoned band looking to optimize your touring strategy, overcoming logistics and scheduling hurdles is crucial to ensure a successful and stress-free experience. From coordinating travel and accommodations to managing tight schedules, there are many moving parts to consider. In this blog post, we'll explore practical tips and strategies to help you efficiently plan your tour, overcome common challenges, and keep everything running smoothly.

The Importance of Efficient Tour Planning

MAXIMIZING YOUR REACH

One of the primary goals of touring is to reach as many fans as possible. Efficient tour planning allows you to maximize your reach by carefully selecting cities and venues that align with your fanbase. By optimizing your route and schedule, you can perform in more locations without overextending yourself or your team.

Minimizing Costs

Touring can be expensive, with costs for transportation, lodging, meals, and more quickly adding up. Effective planning helps you minimize these costs by identifying the most cost-effective options for travel, accommodation, and other expenses. This allows you to make the most of your budget while still delivering an exceptional experience for your fans.

Ensuring Smooth Operations

A well-planned tour ensures that everything runs smoothly, from load-ins to soundchecks to performances. By addressing logistical challenges ahead of time, you reduce the risk of delays, miscommunications, and other issues that could disrupt your tour. This helps you stay focused on what really matters: delivering great performances and connecting with your audience.

Common Logistics and Scheduling Hurdles

VENUE AVAILABILITY

One of the most significant challenges in tour planning is securing venues that align with your schedule. Popular venues often book up months in advance, making it difficult to find available dates that fit your tour plan.

Travel Coordination

Coordinating travel between cities can be a logistical nightmare. You need to consider the distance between locations, travel time, and the most efficient modes of transportation. Additionally, unexpected issues like traffic, weather, or vehicle breakdowns can throw a wrench in your plans.

Accommodation Challenges

Finding suitable accommodations for your team can be tricky, especially when working with a tight budget. You need to ensure that your team has a comfortable place to rest and recharge after each performance, without breaking the bank.

Scheduling Conflicts

Scheduling conflicts can arise at any time, whether it's a double booking, an unplanned event, or a member of your team having a prior commitment. These conflicts can disrupt your tour and require last-minute adjustments.

Health and Well-being of the Team

Touring can be physically and mentally exhausting. Long hours on the road, irregular sleep schedules, and the demands of performing can take a toll on your team's health and well-being. It's important to plan for rest days and consider the well-being of everyone involved.

Steps to Overcome Tour Planning Hurdles

STEP 1: START PLANNING Early

The earlier you start planning your tour, the better. This gives you more time to secure venues, coordinate travel, and address any potential issues before they become critical. Ideally, start planning at least six months before your intended tour dates.

Step 2: Optimize Your Route

When planning your tour route, consider the geography of your locations to minimize travel time and costs. Group nearby cities together and plan your route in a logical, efficient manner. This not only reduces travel expenses but also minimizes wear and tear on your team.

Step 3: Work with a Reliable Booking Agent

A reliable booking agent can be invaluable in securing venues and managing the logistics of your tour. They have industry connections and experience that can help you navigate the complexities of tour planning. If you don't already have a booking agent, consider hiring one to assist with your tour.

Step 4: Budget Wisely

Create a detailed budget that accounts for all potential expenses, including travel, accommodations, food, equipment, and contingencies. Stick to your budget as closely as possible to avoid financial strain. Look for ways to save money, such as booking group accommodations or using loyalty programs for travel.

Step 5: Use Tour Planning Software

There are several tour planning software options available that can help streamline the logistics of your tour. These tools allow you to manage your schedule, track expenses, and coordinate with your team all in one place. Some popular options include Master Tour and Eventric's LiveTour.

Step 6: Have Backup Plans

Always have backup plans in place for key aspects of your tour, such as alternative routes, backup accommodations, and contingency funds. This ensures that you're prepared for unexpected challenges, such as a venue canceling at the last minute or a vehicle breakdown.

Step 7: Prioritize Communication

Clear and consistent communication with your team, venues, and other stakeholders is essential for a successful tour. Use communication tools like group chats, project management apps, and regular meetings to keep everyone on the same page.

Step 8: Plan for Health and Wellness

Schedule rest days throughout your tour to give your team time to recuperate. Encourage healthy eating, regular exercise, and adequate sleep to maintain everyone's well-being. Consider the mental health of your team as well, and provide support when needed.

Benefits of Efficient Tour Planning

REDUCED STRESS

Efficient tour planning reduces stress for everyone involved. By having a clear plan and addressing potential challenges ahead of time, you can focus on delivering great performances rather than worrying about logistics.

Better Audience Engagement

When your tour is well-organized, you can focus more on engaging with your audience and delivering memorable performances. This leads to a better experience for your fans and can help you build a stronger connection with your audience.

Increased Profitability

By minimizing costs and maximizing efficiency, you can increase the profitability of your tour. This allows you to reinvest in your music, grow your brand, and plan even more successful tours in the future.

Enhanced Team Morale

A well-planned tour keeps your team motivated and energized. When everyone knows what to expect and feels supported, morale stays high, leading to better performances and a more positive experience overall.

Conclusion

TOUR PLANNING IS A complex process that requires careful consideration of logistics, scheduling, and the well-being of your team. By starting early, optimizing your route, working with a reliable booking agent, and using the right tools, you can overcome common hurdles and ensure a successful tour. Remember to prioritize communication, plan for contingencies, and focus on the health and wellness of your team. With the right approach, you can efficiently plan your tour, deliver unforgettable performances, and connect with fans across the globe.

FAQs

FAQ 1: HOW EARLY SHOULD I start planning my tour?

Ideally, you should start planning your tour at least six months in advance. This gives you enough time to secure venues, coordinate travel, and address any potential issues.

FAQ 2: What are some tips for minimizing tour costs?

To minimize tour costs, optimize your route to reduce travel expenses, book group accommodations, use loyalty programs for travel, and stick to a detailed budget.

FAQ 3: How can I handle last-minute venue cancellations?

Always have backup plans in place, such as alternative venues or flexible travel arrangements. Work closely with your booking agent to find solutions quickly.

FAQ 4: What should I include in my tour budget?

Your tour budget should include expenses for travel, accommodations, food, equipment, insurance, and contingency funds for unexpected costs.

FAQ 5: How can I maintain my team's health and well-being on tour?

Schedule rest days, encourage healthy eating, regular exercise, and adequate sleep, and provide mental health support when needed.

Best Practices for a Successful Sound Check

A thorough sound check is essential for ensuring that your performance or recording session runs smoothly. It allows you to identify and resolve any audio issues before they become problems during your performance. Whether you're preparing for a live show or a recording session, following these best practices for a successful sound check will help you achieve the best possible sound.

1. Arrive Early and Be Prepared

- TIMING: ARRIVE AT the venue or studio well before the scheduled start time to allow ample time for setup and troubleshooting. Rushing through a sound check increases the likelihood of missing crucial details.

- Preparation: Bring all necessary equipment, including instruments, microphones, cables, and any personal gear like pedals or stands. Ensure everything is in working order before the sound check begins.

2. Communicate with the Sound Engineer

- INTRODUCTION: INTRODUCE yourself to the sound engineer and discuss any specific requirements or preferences you have for your sound.

- Feedback: Provide clear feedback during the sound check, but also be open to the engineer's suggestions. They are there to help you achieve the best sound possible.

3. Start with a Line Check

- CHECK EACH INPUT: Begin by checking each input individually (microphones, instruments, etc.). Ensure that every channel is receiving a clear signal and that there are no issues like crackling cables or faulty connections.
    - Level Setting: Set the initial levels for each channel, making sure that nothing is too quiet or too loud. This will provide a solid foundation for the rest of the sound check.

4. Balance the Mix

- GROUP SOUND CHECK: After the line check, have the entire band or ensemble play together to balance the overall mix. Ensure that no single instrument or vocal overpowers the others.
    - Volume Levels: Pay attention to the volume levels between instruments and vocals. The goal is to create a balanced mix where every element is clearly heard.

5. Monitor Placement and Levels

- MONITOR PLACEMENT: Ensure that stage monitors are positioned correctly so that each performer can hear themselves and the other instruments clearly.
    - Monitor Levels: Adjust the levels in the monitors according to each performer's needs. This is crucial for ensuring that everyone can perform confidently without straining to hear.

6. Test Different Sections of the Performance

- QUIET AND LOUD SECTIONS: Test both the quietest and loudest parts of your set to ensure that the sound remains clear and balanced throughout. This helps prevent surprises during the actual performance.

- Special Effects: If you're using any effects, like reverb or delay, test them during the sound check to make sure they're set up correctly and won't cause any issues during the performance.

7. Check for Feedback

- MICROPHONE FEEDBACK: Test each microphone for feedback by walking around the stage with the mic turned on. Adjust the placement, gain, or EQ settings to eliminate any potential feedback issues.
- Speaker Placement: Ensure that the speakers are positioned to minimize the chance of feedback. Angle them away from microphones and reflective surfaces like walls.

8. Test the Room Acoustics

- ROOM SOUND: PAY ATTENTION to how the room itself affects the sound. Large, empty rooms might create echoes, while smaller, crowded spaces might absorb too much sound. Adjust your levels and EQ to compensate for the room's acoustics.
- Audience Simulation: If possible, simulate the presence of an audience (e.g., by placing some people in the room) to get a more accurate sense of how the sound will behave when the venue is full.

9. Final Walkthrough

- STAGE CHECK: WALK around the stage and listen from different positions to ensure that the sound is consistent throughout. This helps catch any anomalies that might not be noticeable from a single location.

- Final Adjustments: Make any final adjustments to the mix, monitor levels, or EQ settings based on what you hear during the walkthrough.

10. Document the Settings

- TAKE NOTES: DOCUMENT the settings for each channel, including gain, EQ, effects, and monitor levels. This is particularly important if you'll be performing multiple shows or sessions in the same venue.
- Save the Mix: If you're using a digital mixing console, save the mix settings so they can be recalled easily for future performances.

Conclusion

A SUCCESSFUL SOUND check sets the stage for a smooth and professional performance. By arriving early, communicating effectively, and thoroughly testing your equipment, you can identify and resolve any issues before they become a problem. Remember, a well-executed sound check is not just about technical adjustments—it's about creating an environment where you can perform confidently, knowing that your sound will be the best it can be.

Which Strings Stay In Tune The Longest: Nylon or Steel?

When it comes to choosing between nylon and steel strings, one of the key considerations for many guitarists is tuning stability. Whether you're playing a classical guitar with nylon strings or an acoustic/electric guitar with steel strings, keeping your instrument in tune is crucial for consistent sound quality. But do steel or nylon strings stay in tune longest? Let's dive into the characteristics of both nylon and steel strings to find out.

Nylon Strings: Pros and Cons

NYLON STRINGS ARE COMMONLY used on classical guitars and are known for their warm, mellow tone. They are made from synthetic materials like nylon, fluorocarbon, or a combination of these, and are often favored by classical, flamenco, and fingerstyle guitarists.

Tuning Stability of Nylon Strings

- Stretching Period: Nylon strings generally have a longer stretching period when first installed. This means they may take several days to settle in and hold their tuning reliably. During this time, you might find yourself needing to retune frequently.

- Temperature and Humidity Sensitivity: Nylon strings are more sensitive to changes in temperature and humidity compared to steel strings. These environmental factors can cause nylon strings to expand or contract, leading to fluctuations in tuning.

- Long-Term Stability: Once nylon strings have settled in, they tend to hold their tuning relatively well, especially if the guitar is stored in a stable environment. However, they are still more prone to minor tuning shifts due to their sensitivity to environmental changes.

Steel Strings: Pros and Cons

STEEL STRINGS ARE THE go-to choice for most acoustic, electric, and even some hybrid guitars. They produce a bright, crisp sound with more volume and sustain compared to nylon strings, making them popular among rock, blues, and country players.

Tuning Stability of Steel Strings

- Initial Stability: Steel strings have a shorter stretching period than nylon strings. They usually settle in more quickly and begin to hold their tuning better after just a few hours of playing.

- Durability: Steel strings are generally more durable than nylon strings, which contributes to their tuning stability. They are less affected by temperature and humidity changes, making them more reliable in various environments.

- Long-Term Stability: Over time, steel strings maintain their tuning better than nylon strings, especially under heavy playing conditions. However, as they age, they can lose their intonation and tuning stability, particularly if they become corroded or worn.

Factors That Influence Tuning Stability

REGARDLESS OF WHETHER you use nylon or steel strings, several factors can influence tuning stability:

- String Gauge: Heavier gauge strings tend to stay in tune better than lighter ones, but they may require more effort to play.

- String Quality: High-quality strings, whether nylon or steel, are less prone to stretching and tuning issues.

- Tuning Pegs: The quality of your guitar's tuning pegs and their proper maintenance can also affect how well your strings stay in tune.

- Playing Style: Aggressive playing, frequent bending, and using a capo can all cause strings to go out of tune more quickly.

Which Strings Stay in Tune the Longest?

IN GENERAL, STEEL STRINGS tend to stay in tune longer than nylon strings. Their shorter stretching period, greater resistance to environmental factors, and overall durability make them more stable in terms of tuning. However, the best choice ultimately depends on your playing style, the type of music you play, and the sound you prefer.

Final Thoughts

IF TUNING STABILITY is your top priority and you play music that demands precise intonation, steel strings are likely the better option for you. On the other hand, if you prefer the softer, warmer tone of nylon strings and are willing to invest a bit more time in maintaining tuning, nylon strings can also be a great choice.

Understanding the strengths and weaknesses of both nylon and steel strings will help you make an informed decision based on your needs as a musician. Whether you choose nylon or steel, ensuring that your guitar is well-maintained and your strings are of high quality will go a long way in keeping your instrument in tune and sounding its best.

Leveraging Analytics for Music Industry Success

In today's music industry, data isn't just a buzzword—it's a powerful tool that can unlock the doors to growth and success. With the vast array of analytics tools available, artists have access to detailed insights about their audience, streaming performance, and social media engagement. But how do you make sense of all this data? This guide will help you with leveraging analytics for music industry success and use it to fuel your growth.

1. Why Music Analytics Matter

MUSIC ANALYTICS PROVIDE a window into how your music is performing and who your audience is. Understanding these metrics helps you make informed decisions about your career, from marketing strategies to tour planning. Instead of guessing what works, you can rely on data to guide your choices, leading to more targeted efforts and better results.

2. Key Metrics to Monitor

WHILE THERE ARE COUNTLESS data points available, certain metrics are particularly valuable for musicians. Here are a few to focus on:

- Streaming Numbers: Track how many streams your songs are getting on platforms like Spotify, Apple Music, and YouTube. Pay attention to which songs are performing best and where your streams are coming from geographically.

- Audience Demographics: Understanding the age, gender, location, and interests of your audience helps you tailor your content and marketing efforts. Are you reaching your target demographic? If not, how can you adjust your approach?

- Engagement Rates: Measure how actively your fans are engaging with your content. This includes likes, comments, shares, and saves on social media, as well as interaction with your newsletters or website.

- Growth Trends: Look at how your followers, subscribers, and streams are growing over time. Consistent upward trends indicate that your efforts are working, while plateaus or declines might signal a need for a strategy shift.

3. Popular Analytics Tools for Musicians

SEVERAL PLATFORMS OFFER robust analytics tools specifically designed for musicians. Here are a few of the most popular:

- Spotify for Artists: This platform provides detailed insights into your streaming data, including real-time stats, audience demographics, and playlist placements. Use it to track your most popular songs and see how fans are discovering your music.

- YouTube Analytics: YouTube's analytics tool gives you a deep dive into video performance, watch time, audience retention, and traffic sources. Understanding which videos are most effective can help you create more engaging content.

- Social Media Insights (Instagram, Facebook, Twitter): Each social media platform has its own analytics tools that provide information on engagement, reach, and audience demographics. These insights can guide your content creation and posting schedule.

- Google Analytics: If you have a website, Google Analytics is invaluable for tracking visitor behavior, referral sources, and conversion rates. It helps you understand how fans are interacting with your site and what drives them to take action.

4. How to Interpret Your Data

INTERPRETING DATA IS where the real magic happens. Here's how to make sense of the numbers:

- Look for Patterns: Identify trends over time. Are certain songs consistently outperforming others? Is there a spike in streams after specific promotional efforts? Patterns can reveal what's working and what isn't.

- Segment Your Audience: Break down your data by different audience segments. For example, compare the behavior of fans in different countries or age groups. This can help you tailor your strategies to different segments more effectively.

- Compare Against Benchmarks: Set benchmarks based on your past performance or industry standards. Are you growing faster or slower than expected? Use these comparisons to set realistic goals and measure progress.

- Analyze Drop-Off Points: In video analytics, pay attention to when viewers are dropping off. This can indicate when content becomes less engaging and help you refine your approach.

5. Using Data to Drive Growth

ONCE YOU'VE INTERPRETED your data, it's time to put it to use. Here's how:

- Optimize Your Content: Use insights to create more of what your audience loves. If certain types of posts, videos, or songs perform better, focus on producing more of that content.

- Target Your Marketing: Tailor your marketing efforts based on audience demographics and engagement data. For example, if you notice a strong following in a particular city, consider planning a tour stop there or running location-specific ads.

- Adjust Your Strategy: If your data shows that certain efforts aren't yielding results, don't be afraid to pivot. Data-driven decisions are more likely to lead to success than sticking with a strategy that isn't working.

- Set SMART Goals: Use your data to set Specific, Measurable, Achievable, Relevant, and Time-bound (SMART) goals. For example, you might aim to increase your streaming numbers by 20% over the next six months or double your social media engagement by the end of the year.

Conclusion

MUSIC ANALYTICS CAN seem overwhelming at first, but once you understand how to interpret and apply the data, it becomes an invaluable tool for growth. By focusing on key metrics, using the right tools, and making data-driven decisions, you can take your music career to new heights. Remember, the numbers are there to guide you—use them to your advantage, and watch your fanbase and success grow.

Fan Demographics: Analyzing Data for Targeted Marketing

Introduction

UNDERSTANDING YOUR audience is the cornerstone of effective marketing. Whether you're a musician, content creator, or business owner, knowing who your fans are allows you to tailor your messaging, products, and services to meet their needs and preferences. This is where fan demographics come into play. By analyzing demographic data, you can gain valuable insights into your audience's age, gender, location, interests, and more. In this blog post, we'll explore the importance of fan demographics, discuss how to analyze this data, and provide strategies for using it to create targeted marketing campaigns that resonate with your audience.

The Importance of Understanding Fan Demographics

PERSONALIZED MARKETING

One of the biggest advantages of understanding fan demographics is the ability to create personalized marketing campaigns. When you know who your fans are, you can craft messages that speak directly to them, addressing their specific interests, needs, and pain points. This level of personalization can lead to higher engagement rates, increased loyalty, and ultimately, more conversions.

Optimized Content Creation

Content creation is at the heart of any successful marketing strategy. By analyzing fan demographics, you can determine what type of content resonates most with your audience. For example, if your fan base consists mainly of younger individuals, you might focus on creating content that's more visual and shareable on platforms like Instagram or TikTok. On the other hand, if your audience is older, you might prioritize long-form content and educational resources.

Efficient Ad Spend

When you understand your audience, you can allocate your ad budget more effectively. Instead of casting a wide net and hoping for the best, targeted marketing allows you to focus your resources on the platforms, channels, and demographics that are most likely to convert. This not only saves you money but also increases the return on investment (ROI) for your marketing efforts.

Better Product Development

Fan demographics can also inform product development. By understanding the preferences and behaviors of your audience, you can create products and services that are more likely to meet their needs and desires. This can lead to higher customer satisfaction and more repeat business.

Key Fan Demographics to Analyze

AGE

Age is one of the most important demographics to consider. Different age groups have different preferences, behaviors, and spending habits. For example, younger fans might be more interested in social media interactions and digital products, while older fans might prefer traditional media and physical goods.

Gender

Gender can also play a significant role in shaping your marketing strategy. By understanding the gender distribution of your audience, you can create campaigns that resonate with specific groups. For instance, if your fan base is predominantly female, you might focus on themes and messaging that appeal to women.

Location

Geographical data is crucial for understanding where your fans are located. This can help you tailor your marketing efforts to specific regions, cities, or even neighborhoods. Location data can also inform decisions about where to host events, how to price products, and which markets to target next.

Interests and Hobbies

Understanding your fans' interests and hobbies allows you to create content and products that align with their passions. For example, if a large portion of your audience is interested in fitness, you might create content that ties your brand to healthy living or active lifestyles.

Income Level

Income level can influence purchasing decisions and should be considered when pricing products or creating marketing campaigns. If your audience has a higher income, they might be more interested in premium products and services. Conversely, if your audience has a lower income, you might focus on affordability and value.

Education Level

Education level can provide insights into the type of content and messaging that will resonate with your audience. For example, a more educated audience might prefer detailed, data-driven content, while a less educated audience might respond better to simple, straightforward messaging.

How to Gather and Analyze Fan Demographics

STEP 1: USE SOCIAL Media Analytics

Social media platforms like Facebook, Instagram, and Twitter offer built-in analytics tools that provide demographic data about your followers. These tools can give you insights into the age, gender, location, and interests of your audience. Regularly reviewing these analytics can help you stay informed about who your fans are and how they're engaging with your content.

Step 2: Conduct Surveys and Polls

Surveys and polls are effective ways to gather demographic data directly from your audience. You can ask questions about age, gender, location, interests, and more. Tools like Google Forms, SurveyMonkey, and social media polls make it easy to create and distribute surveys to your fans.

Step 3: Analyze Website Traffic Data

Tools like Google Analytics provide detailed information about the demographics of your website visitors. You can see data on age, gender, location, and even the devices and browsers your audience is using. This information can help you understand who's visiting your site and how they're interacting with your content.

Step 4: Monitor Purchase Data

If you're selling products or services, analyzing purchase data can give you valuable insights into your audience's demographics. Look at the age, gender, and location of your customers, as well as their purchasing habits. This can help you identify trends and tailor your offerings to better meet their needs.

Step 5: Use Third-Party Data Providers

There are many third-party data providers that can help you gather demographic information about your audience. These services often aggregate data from various sources to provide a more comprehensive view of your audience. Some popular options include Nielsen, Comscore, and Experian.

Strategies for Targeted Marketing Based on Demographics

CREATE SEGMENTED CAMPAIGNS

One of the most effective ways to use demographic data is to create segmented marketing campaigns. By dividing your audience into smaller groups based on age, gender, location, or interests, you can create more personalized and relevant messaging. For example, you might create separate email campaigns for different age groups, with each campaign highlighting products or content that's most likely to appeal to that group.

Tailor Your Content Strategy

Use demographic data to inform your content strategy. If your audience is predominantly young, focus on creating content that's visually engaging and easily shareable. If your audience is older, you might prioritize more in-depth articles, videos, and educational content. Tailoring your content to the preferences of your audience can lead to higher engagement and more meaningful connections with your fans.

Optimize Your Ad Targeting

Demographic data is invaluable when it comes to ad targeting. Platforms like Facebook and Google Ads allow you to target ads based on age, gender, location, interests, and more. By using this data to refine your ad targeting, you can ensure that your ads are being seen by the people who are most likely to engage with them.

Personalize Your Messaging

Personalization is key to effective marketing. Use demographic data to create personalized messages that speak directly to your audience's needs and interests. Whether it's through email marketing, social media, or direct mail, personalized messaging can increase engagement and build stronger relationships with your fans.

Adjust Your Pricing and Promotions

Consider the income level and purchasing habits of your audience when setting prices and creating promotions. If your audience is price-sensitive, you might offer discounts, bundles, or loyalty programs to encourage purchases. On the other hand, if your audience values premium products, you might focus on highlighting the quality and exclusivity of your offerings.

Conclusion

UNDERSTANDING FAN DEMOGRAPHICS is essential for creating targeted marketing campaigns that resonate with your audience. By analyzing data on age, gender, location, interests, and more, you can gain valuable insights into who your fans are and what they want. This knowledge allows you to personalize your marketing efforts, optimize your content strategy, and allocate your resources more effectively. Start by gathering demographic data using social media analytics, surveys, website traffic data, and purchase data. Then, use this information to create segmented campaigns, tailor your content, and refine your ad targeting. With a deep understanding of your audience, you can create marketing campaigns that truly connect with your fans and drive meaningful results.

FAQs

FAQ 1: WHAT ARE FAN demographics?

Fan demographics refer to the statistical characteristics of your audience, such as age, gender, location, interests, income level, and education. Understanding these demographics helps you tailor your marketing efforts to better connect with your audience.

FAQ 2: How can I gather demographic data about my audience?

You can gather demographic data using social media analytics, surveys, website traffic tools like Google Analytics, purchase data, and third-party data providers.

FAQ 3: Why is it important to understand fan demographics?

Understanding fan demographics allows you to create personalized marketing campaigns, optimize content, allocate your ad budget more effectively, and develop products that meet your audience's needs.

FAQ 4: How can I use fan demographics for targeted marketing?

Use fan demographics to create segmented campaigns, tailor your content strategy, optimize ad targeting, personalize your messaging, and adjust pricing and promotions based on your audience's preferences.

FAQ 5: What tools can help me analyze fan demographics?

Tools like Google Analytics, social media analytics platforms, SurveyMonkey, and third-party data providers like Nielsen and Comscore can help you analyze fan demographics and gain valuable insights into your audience.

Music Video Storyboarding: Solving Visual Narrative Challenges

Introduction to Music Video Storyboarding

IN THE WORLD OF MUSIC videos, visuals play an equally important role as the music itself. But creating compelling visuals isn't just about picking up a camera and shooting; it starts with a solid plan. That's where storyboarding comes in. Storyboarding is the art of planning out each scene, shot, and visual element of a music video, ensuring that the final product is cohesive, engaging, and in sync with the music. But storyboarding isn't without its challenges, especially when it comes to translating abstract ideas into a visual narrative. This article will dive into the importance of storyboarding in music videos and explore how to solve common visual narrative challenges.

Understanding the Basics of Storyboarding

WHAT IS A STORYBOARD?

A storyboard is a visual representation of how a music video will unfold, shot by shot. It's essentially a series of drawings that show how each scene will look, including camera angles, movements, and transitions. Think of it as a comic strip, but with a focus on planning out every detail of the music video. Each frame of the storyboard serves as a guide for the production team, helping to visualize the final product before any filming begins.

Key Elements of an Effective Storyboard

VISUALIZING SCENES

One of the main purposes of a storyboard is to visualize scenes before they are filmed. This involves breaking down the song into different parts and determining how each part will be represented visually. It's about thinking through every moment and deciding what will be seen on screen and how it will connect with the music.

Detailing Camera Angles and Movements

A well-thought-out storyboard includes specific details about camera angles and movements. Will the camera be stationary, or will it follow the subject? Will there be close-ups or wide shots? These decisions impact how the audience experiences the music video and must be carefully planned out in the storyboard.

Integrating the Music and Lyrics

The visuals in a music video need to align with the music and lyrics. This integration is a critical part of storyboarding. Whether it's a literal interpretation of the lyrics or a more abstract representation, the storyboard should reflect how the visuals will enhance the music and convey the intended message or emotion.

Identifying Common Visual Narrative Challenges

CHALLENGE 1: TRANSLATING Abstract Concepts into Visuals

Music videos often deal with abstract concepts, such as emotions, ideas, or themes that aren't easy to depict visually. Translating these abstract concepts into a visual narrative is one of the biggest challenges in storyboarding. It requires creativity, imagination, and a deep understanding of the song's message.

Challenge 2: Ensuring Cohesiveness in the Storyline

Another challenge is ensuring that the music video tells a cohesive story from start to finish. This involves maintaining a consistent tone, style, and flow throughout the video. A disjointed or confusing narrative can detract from the impact of the video, so it's crucial to map out the storyline in the storyboard.

Challenge 3: Balancing Artistic Vision with Practical Constraints

While creativity is key, practical constraints like budget and time often limit what can be achieved. Balancing artistic vision with these constraints is a common challenge in music video production.

Budgetary Limitations

A GRAND VISION MAY require expensive locations, props, or special effects that aren't feasible within the available budget. Storyboarding helps identify where compromises can be made without sacrificing the overall vision.

Time Constraints

Time is another factor that can impact the storyboarding process. Tight deadlines may mean that certain shots or scenes need to be simplified or cut altogether. Storyboarding allows for careful planning to ensure that the video can be completed on time.

Challenge 4: Capturing Audience Emotion and Attention

Finally, a major challenge in music video storyboarding is creating visuals that capture the audience's emotion and attention. The visuals should not only complement the music but also evoke the intended emotional response from the audience.

Step-by-Step Guide to Effective Music Video Storyboarding

STEP 1: ANALYZING THE Song's Lyrics and Theme

The first step in storyboarding a music video is to analyze the song's lyrics and theme. This involves understanding the message, emotion, and mood that the song conveys. Once you have a clear grasp of the song's essence, you can start brainstorming visual ideas that align with the music.

Step 2: Brainstorming Visual Ideas

After analyzing the song, the next step is brainstorming visual ideas. This is where creativity comes into play. Consider different ways to represent the song's message visually. Will you go for a literal interpretation of the lyrics, or will you use metaphors and symbolism to convey the theme?

Collaborating with the Creative Team

Brainstorming is often a collaborative process that involves input from the director, cinematographer, and other members of the creative team. Collaboration ensures that all ideas are considered and that the final storyboard reflects a unified vision.

Step 3: Sketching the Storyboard Frames

Once you have a clear idea of the visuals, it's time to start sketching the storyboard frames. Each frame should represent a specific moment in the music video, including details about the camera angle, movement, and transition.

Using Storyboarding Software vs. Hand-drawn Sketches

There are different ways to create a storyboard, from traditional hand-drawn sketches to digital storyboarding software. Both methods have their advantages. Hand-drawn sketches offer a more personal touch, while digital tools provide more precision and flexibility.

Step 4: Reviewing and Refining the Storyboard

Storyboarding is an iterative process, meaning that it often involves multiple drafts and revisions. After the initial sketches are done, it's important to review and refine the storyboard to ensure that it effectively communicates the intended visual narrative.

Step 5: Finalizing the Storyboard for Production

The final step in the storyboarding process is to finalize the storyboard for production. This involves making any last-minute adjustments and ensuring that the storyboard is clear and detailed enough to guide the production team during filming.

Tools and Techniques for Storyboarding

POPULAR STORYBOARDING Software for Music Videos

There are several software options available for creating storyboards, each with its unique features. Popular choices include Adobe Storyboard, Storyboarder, and Toon Boom Storyboard Pro. These tools offer a range of functionalities, from basic sketching to advanced animation and collaboration features.

Traditional Storyboarding Techniques

Pencil and Paper

For those who prefer a more traditional approach, pencil and paper are still a popular choice for storyboarding. This method allows for quick

sketches and is often favored by those with strong drawing skills.

Digital Tools

Digital tools, on the other hand, offer greater flexibility and the ability to make changes easily. Many digital storyboarding programs also come with pre-made templates and assets, making it easier to create detailed and professional-looking storyboards.

Conclusion

RECAP OF STORYBOARDING Importance in Music Videos

Storyboarding is a vital part of the music video production process. It serves as a blueprint that guides the entire production, ensuring that the final product is visually engaging, cohesive, and in sync with the music.

Final Thoughts on Overcoming Visual Narrative Challenges

While storyboarding comes with its challenges, from translating abstract concepts into visuals to balancing artistic vision with practical constraints, it is an essential tool for overcoming these obstacles. With careful planning and creativity, you can create a music video that not only tells a compelling story but also resonates with your audience.

FAQs

FAQ 1: WHAT IS THE most challenging part of music video storyboarding?

The most challenging part is often translating abstract concepts and emotions into visual elements that are both engaging and understandable.

FAQ 2: How long does it take to storyboard a music video?

The time it takes can vary depending on the complexity of the video, but it typically ranges from a few days to several weeks.

FAQ 3: Can I create a storyboard without professional software?

Yes, you can create a storyboard using traditional methods like pencil and paper, or you can use free digital tools if professional software is not accessible.

FAQ 4: How detailed should a music video storyboard be?

A storyboard should be detailed enough to guide the production team through each shot and scene, but it doesn't need to be overly complex.

FAQ 5: What are the key skills needed for effective storyboarding?

Key skills include creativity, attention to detail, an understanding of visual storytelling, and the ability to translate ideas into visual form.

Understanding Microphone Feedback and How to Avoid It

Microphone feedback is one of the most common and frustrating issues faced by musicians, speakers, and audio engineers. That high-pitched screech or loud hum can disrupt a performance, irritate the audience, and leave you scrambling to fix the problem. Fortunately, by understanding the causes of microphone feedback and implementing a few strategies, you can significantly reduce or eliminate it altogether.

What is Microphone Feedback?

MICROPHONE FEEDBACK occurs when a microphone picks up sound from a speaker that is amplified and sent back through the speaker again, creating a loop. This loop amplifies the sound repeatedly, resulting in the unpleasant noise known as feedback.

Common Causes of Microphone Feedback

1. PROXIMITY OF MICROPHONE to Speaker: The closer the microphone is to the speaker, the more likely it is to pick up sound from the speaker and create a feedback loop.

2. Microphone Gain: If the gain (sensitivity) on the microphone is too high, it will pick up more sound from its surroundings, increasing the chances of feedback.

3. Poor Room Acoustics: Certain environments, especially those with reflective surfaces, can cause sound to bounce around and increase the likelihood of feedback.

4. Improper Speaker Placement: If speakers are positioned in such a way that they project sound directly towards the microphone, feedback is more likely to occur.

How to Avoid Microphone Feedback

1. POSITION YOUR MICROPHONE and Speakers Strategically: Keep microphones as far away from speakers as possible and avoid pointing the microphone directly at any speakers. Angling speakers away from the microphone and towards the audience can help prevent feedback.

2. Lower the Microphone Gain: Reduce the gain on your microphone to minimize the amount of ambient sound it picks up. You want the microphone to capture your voice or instrument clearly, without picking up unnecessary background noise.

3. Use a Directional Microphone: Directional microphones, such as cardioid or supercardioid mics, are designed to pick up sound from a specific direction. This helps to reduce the likelihood of feedback by minimizing the amount of sound the microphone picks up from the speakers or other sources.

4. Utilize EQ to Cut Problem Frequencies: Feedback often occurs at specific frequencies. By using an equalizer (EQ) to identify and reduce those frequencies, you can prevent feedback. A technique known as "notching" involves cutting the frequency bands where feedback is most likely to occur.

5. Use a Feedback Eliminator: Feedback eliminators are devices or software that automatically detect and suppress feedback frequencies. They can be particularly useful in complex audio setups or environments prone to feedback.

6. Adjust the Room Acoustics: If possible, improve the acoustics of the room where you're performing. Adding sound-absorbing materials

like curtains, carpets, or acoustic panels can help reduce reflections and the likelihood of feedback.

7. Monitor Levels Carefully: Keep an eye on the levels of your audio equipment, including the microphone, mixer, and speakers. Ensure that no single component is overly amplified, as this can contribute to feedback.

8. Perform a Sound Check: Before your performance, always conduct a thorough sound check to identify any potential feedback issues. Walk around the space with the microphone to see if any areas are particularly prone to feedback, and make adjustments as needed.

Conclusion

MICROPHONE FEEDBACK is a common challenge, but with the right techniques, it can be managed effectively. By positioning your equipment strategically, adjusting settings, and using the right tools, you can minimize the chances of feedback and ensure a smooth performance. Remember, a little preparation goes a long way in creating a professional and pleasant audio experience for both you and your audience.

Essential Monitor EQ Tips: Equalizing Onstage Monitors For Clear Sound

Properly Equalizing your onstage monitors is crucial for ensuring that you and your fellow performers can hear everything clearly during a live performance. When your monitor mix is well-balanced, you can focus on your performance without straining to hear yourself or other band members. Here are some essential tips for EQing your monitors to achieve optimal sound on stage.

1. Start with a Flat EQ

- Baseline Settings: Begin with all EQ settings flat (no boosts or cuts). This gives you a neutral starting point from which you can make adjustments based on the specific needs of the stage and performers.

- Adjust Incrementally: Make small, gradual adjustments to the EQ. Large changes can cause drastic shifts in sound, which can be disorienting and difficult to control.

2. Tackle Feedback First

- Identify Problem Frequencies: Feedback often occurs at specific frequencies. Use a parametric EQ to narrow in on the feedback frequency and then reduce it with a notch filter.

- High-Pass Filters: Engage a high-pass filter to remove low-end rumble and sub-bass frequencies that can muddy the monitor mix and contribute to feedback. Set the filter around 80-100 Hz, depending on the instrument or vocal.

3. Enhance Clarity

- Cut Muddy Frequencies: In the low-mid range (around 200-500 Hz), excessive energy can cause the mix to sound muddy. Gently cut these frequencies to clear up the sound, especially for vocals and guitars.

- Boost Presence: To improve clarity and definition, especially for vocals, slightly boost the presence range (around 2-5 kHz). This helps the vocals cut through the mix without being overpowering.

4. Balance the High Frequencies

- Avoid Harshness: High frequencies (above 10 kHz) can sometimes be harsh or piercing in monitors. If the sound is too bright or sibilant, slightly reduce these frequencies to create a smoother, more comfortable listening experience.

- Cymbals and High-Hats: For drummers, ensure that cymbals and hi-hats are clear but not overpowering in the mix. A subtle boost around 10 kHz can add brilliance, but too much can lead to ear fatigue.

5. Customize for Each Performer

- Individual Preferences: Every performer has different preferences for their monitor mix. Some may need more bass, while others might require more midrange or treble. Tailor the EQ for each monitor to suit the specific needs of each performer.

- Instrument-Specific EQ: If monitors are dedicated to specific instruments (e.g., a monitor for the drummer or bassist), adjust the EQ to highlight the most critical frequencies for that instrument.

6. Keep the Mix Natural

- Avoid Over-EQing: While it's important to address problem areas, avoid the temptation to over-EQ. Too many cuts and boosts can result in an unnatural sound that's difficult to work with on stage.

- Maintain Tonal Balance: Ensure that the overall tonal balance of the monitor mix remains natural. The goal is to replicate the sound of the instruments and vocals as accurately as possible, with adjustments made only for clarity and feedback control.

7. Test and Adjust On Stage

- Sound Check Adjustments: After setting the initial EQ, test the sound on stage during sound check. Walk around and listen from different positions to ensure consistency in the monitor mix.

- Fine-Tuning: Use the sound check to fine-tune the EQ based on how the monitors sound in the live environment. Make adjustments in real-time and check with the performers to ensure they're comfortable with the sound.

8. Monitor the Volume

- Avoid Excessive Volume: Loud monitors can lead to hearing fatigue and make it difficult to achieve a clean mix. Keep monitor levels at a comfortable volume that allows everyone to hear clearly without overwhelming the stage sound.

- Protect Hearing: Encourage the use of in-ear monitors or earplugs for performers to protect their hearing, especially in loud environments. This can also reduce the need for excessive volume in stage monitors.

Conclusion

EQING YOUR STAGE MONITORS effectively is key to ensuring a clear, balanced, and feedback-free mix that allows performers to hear themselves and each other comfortably. By starting with a flat EQ, addressing feedback, and making careful, purposeful adjustments, you can create a monitor mix that supports a great performance. Remember, the goal is to enhance clarity while maintaining a natural sound, so performers can focus on delivering their best on stage.

Navigating Music Licensing: Sync Deals and Royalties Explained

In today's music industry, licensing has become a critical revenue stream for artists, songwriters, and producers. With the rise of digital media, the demand for music in film, television, advertising, video games, and online content has skyrocketed. Understanding how to navigate music licensing, secure sync deals, and maximize your royalties can open up new opportunities and ensure you get paid for your work. This blog post will guide you through the essentials of music licensing, from understanding sync deals to optimizing your royalty streams.

What is Music Licensing?

MUSIC LICENSING IS the process of granting permission to use a piece of music in various forms of media. When you license your music, you allow another party (such as a filmmaker, advertiser, or game developer) to use your composition or recording in exchange for compensation, which often comes in the form of upfront fees, royalties, or both.

There are two main types of music licenses:

1. Master License: This license is needed to use a specific recording of a song. The owner of the master recording, usually the record label or the artist themselves, grants this license.

2. Synchronization License (Sync License): This license allows music to be synchronized with visual media—like a song playing during a scene in a movie or a commercial. The sync license is typically granted by the publisher or songwriter who owns the composition.

Understanding Sync Deals

A SYNCHRONIZATION DEAL, commonly known as a sync deal, is when your music is licensed to be used in sync with visual content. Sync deals are one of the most lucrative forms of music licensing because they can provide both upfront payments and long-term royalties.

How Sync Deals Work:

1. Placement Opportunities: Sync opportunities arise in various media, including TV shows, movies, commercials, video games, trailers, and online content. The music supervisor (the person responsible for selecting and licensing music) identifies a song that fits the project's needs.

2. Negotiating the Deal: If a music supervisor or producer wants to use your music, they'll negotiate a sync fee. This fee can vary widely depending on the budget of the project, the popularity of the song, and the usage (e.g., background music vs. featured song).

3. Upfront Payment: Once the terms are agreed upon, you'll receive an upfront payment for the use of your music. This fee compensates you for allowing your song to be used in the specific project.

4. Backend Royalties: In addition to the upfront payment, you may also earn performance royalties whenever the content is broadcast on TV, streamed online, or shown in theaters. These royalties are typically collected and distributed by Performance Rights Organizations (PROs) like ASCAP, BMI, or SESAC.

Benefits of Sync Deals:

- Exposure: Sync deals can provide significant exposure for your music, potentially reaching millions of viewers or listeners. A well-placed song in a popular TV show, movie, or commercial can lead to increased streams, downloads, and fanbase growth.

- Revenue: Sync deals can be highly lucrative. The upfront fees and ongoing royalties can become a substantial income source, especially if your music is used in major projects or repeatedly licensed.

- Creative Opportunities: Sync placements often involve collaborations with directors, producers, and advertisers, offering creative opportunities to see your music in a new context and reach different audiences.

Navigating Royalties in Music Licensing

WHEN YOUR MUSIC IS licensed, there are several types of royalties you may be entitled to:

1. Mechanical Royalties:

- What They Are: Mechanical royalties are earned when your music is reproduced or distributed, whether physically (like CDs or vinyl) or digitally (like streaming or downloads).

- Who Pays Them: Streaming services, record labels, and other entities that reproduce your music pay these royalties. In the U.S., these are typically collected by organizations like the Harry Fox Agency or through direct deals with the digital platforms.

2. Performance Royalties:

- What They Are: Performance royalties are earned whenever your music is publicly performed or broadcast, including on TV, radio, streaming services, and live venues.

- Who Pays Them: These royalties are collected by Performance Rights Organizations (PROs) such as ASCAP, BMI, and SESAC in the U.S., and by similar organizations internationally. They distribute the royalties to songwriters, composers, and publishers.

3. Sync Royalties:

- What They Are: Sync royalties are paid when your music is used in sync with visual media. They include the upfront sync fee and any additional royalties earned from the content's broadcast.

- Who Pays Them: The upfront fee is paid by the production company or media outlet licensing the music, while performance royalties from the broadcast are collected by PROs.

4. Master Use Royalties:

- What They Are: If you own the master recording of your music, you're entitled to master use royalties whenever that recording is licensed for sync or mechanical uses.

- Who Pays Them: Master use royalties are usually paid by the entity that licenses the recording, such as a film studio or advertising agency.

Tips for Maximizing Licensing Opportunities

1. CREATE SYNC-FRIENDLY Music:

- Understand the Market: Certain types of music are more in demand for sync deals, such as instrumental tracks, emotionally-driven songs, or music that fits specific genres like pop, indie, or cinematic. Research what's trending in sync placements to tailor your music accordingly.

- Produce High-Quality Tracks: Music supervisors look for professionally produced, high-quality tracks. Invest in good production, mixing, and mastering to ensure your music meets industry standards.

2. Build Relationships with Music Supervisors:

- Network: Attend industry events, music conferences, and workshops to connect with music supervisors and licensing professionals. Building relationships can lead to more sync opportunities.

- Pitch Your Music: Proactively pitch your music to music supervisors, sync agencies, and libraries. Make sure your pitches are targeted and include all necessary information, such as links to your tracks, metadata, and licensing terms.

3. Register with PROs and Licensing Agencies:

- Join a PRO: Ensure you're registered with a Performance Rights Organization to collect performance royalties. Choose the one that best fits your needs and location.

- Use Licensing Agencies: Consider partnering with a music licensing agency that specializes in placing music in sync deals. These agencies have established relationships with music supervisors and can help pitch your music to the right projects.

4. Metadata Matters:

- Tag Your Music Properly: Make sure your music files are properly tagged with metadata, including song title, artist name, genre, mood, and contact information. This makes it easier for music supervisors to find and license your tracks.

- Provide Stems and Instrumentals: Offering stems (individual track components) and instrumental versions of your songs can increase their appeal for sync placements, as they allow for more flexibility in how the music is used.

5. Stay Organized:

- Track Your Deals: Keep detailed records of your licensing agreements, royalty payments, and communication with music supervisors. This helps ensure you receive all the royalties you're entitled to and can identify areas for growth.

- Update Your Catalog: Regularly update your music catalog with new releases and make sure all your tracks are easily accessible to potential licensees.

Conclusion

NAVIGATING MUSIC LICENSING, sync deals, and royalties can seem complex, but it's a vital part of building a sustainable music career. By understanding the different types of licenses, negotiating sync deals effectively, and maximizing your royalty streams, you can unlock new revenue opportunities and increase your music's exposure. Remember, the key to success in music licensing lies in creating high-quality, sync-friendly music, building relationships, and staying organized in managing your rights and royalties.

Live Streaming Hacks: Troubleshooting Livestream Issues

Live streaming has become a powerful tool for musicians, content creators, businesses, and anyone looking to connect with their audience in real-time. However, the success of a live stream can be quickly derailed by technical glitches. Nothing is more frustrating than buffering, poor audio quality, or sudden disconnects when you're trying to deliver a live performance or presentation. Fortunately, with the right preparation and troubleshooting livestream issues, you can minimize these issues and ensure a smooth, glitch-free live stream. Here are some essential hacks to keep your live stream running flawlessly.

1. Prepare Your Equipment and Setup

BEFORE YOU GO LIVE, it's crucial to ensure that your equipment and setup are optimized for streaming.

- Check Your Internet Connection: A strong, stable internet connection is the backbone of any live stream. Aim for an upload speed of at least 5 Mbps for standard definition streaming and 10 Mbps or higher for HD quality. Use a wired Ethernet connection instead of Wi-Fi to reduce the risk of drops in connection quality.

- Test Your Equipment: Before going live, thoroughly test your camera, microphone, and any other equipment. Ensure that your camera is producing a clear image, your microphone is capturing clean audio, and all connections are secure.

- Update Software and Firmware: Make sure that all your streaming software, camera, and audio equipment are up to date. Software updates often include bug fixes and performance improvements that can enhance your streaming experience.

2. Optimize Audio Quality

POOR AUDIO QUALITY is a major turnoff for viewers, even more so than low video quality. Here's how to ensure your sound is top-notch.

- Use an External Microphone: Built-in microphones on cameras or laptops often produce subpar audio. Invest in a good quality external microphone, whether it's a USB mic, a lavalier, or a professional condenser mic, to capture clear, crisp sound.

- Eliminate Background Noise: Stream from a quiet environment to minimize background noise. If noise is unavoidable, consider using noise-cancelling software or a microphone with a built-in noise reduction feature.

- Monitor Audio Levels: Use headphones to monitor your audio levels in real-time. This helps you catch and correct issues like clipping, distortion, or overly quiet sound before they ruin your stream.

3. Ensure Stable Video Quality

GLITCHES IN VIDEO QUALITY can distract your audience and make your stream difficult to watch.

- Adjust Bitrate Settings: Bitrate controls the quality of your video stream. If your stream is experiencing lag or buffering, consider lowering the bitrate. A lower bitrate requires less bandwidth and can help maintain a smoother stream.

- Choose the Right Resolution: Streaming at a resolution that your internet connection and equipment can't handle will result in dropped frames and poor video quality. Streaming in 720p is often a good balance between quality and stability if you're facing bandwidth limitations.

- Use a Backup Camera: If possible, have a second camera set up and ready to go in case your primary camera fails. Switching to a backup camera can save your stream if the primary camera encounters issues.

4. Optimize Your Streaming Software

YOUR STREAMING SOFTWARE is the control center for your live stream, so it's important to set it up correctly.

- Use a Reliable Streaming Platform: Whether you're using OBS, Streamlabs, or another software, make sure it's stable and well-suited to your needs. Test different platforms to see which works best with your hardware and streaming style.

- Set Up Scenes in Advance: If your stream involves multiple scenes (e.g., different camera angles, slideshows, or overlays), set them up in your streaming software beforehand. This minimizes the risk of mistakes or delays when switching between scenes during the live stream.

- Enable Stream Delay: If you're concerned about technical glitches or if your content is sensitive, enabling a short stream delay (5-10 seconds) can give you a buffer to address issues before they reach your audience.

5. Manage Your Resources

RESOURCE MANAGEMENT is key to preventing your computer from being overwhelmed during a live stream.

- Close Unnecessary Applications: Streaming is resource-intensive. Close any unnecessary programs or browser tabs to free up your computer's processing power and reduce the risk of your stream crashing.

- Monitor CPU and Memory Usage: Keep an eye on your CPU and memory usage during the stream. If either is consistently high, consider lowering your stream quality or closing additional programs to prevent your system from overheating or freezing.

6. Prepare for Technical Difficulties

NO MATTER HOW WELL you prepare, technical difficulties can still arise. Have a plan in place to deal with them quickly.

- Have a Backup Plan: Create a backup plan for common issues. For example, if your internet connection drops, have a mobile hotspot ready to switch to. If your software crashes, know how to quickly reboot and resume your stream.

- Create a Technical Checklist: Before going live, go through a checklist to ensure everything is in order. This should include checking your internet connection, camera, microphone, streaming software, and any other equipment.

- Communicate with Your Audience: If technical issues do arise, communicate with your audience. Let them know what's happening and what you're doing to fix it. Transparency can help maintain viewer trust even in the face of problems.

7. Test Everything Before Going Live

ONE OF THE BEST WAYS to prevent technical glitches during your live stream is to conduct a thorough test run.

- Run a Private Test Stream: Set up a private or unlisted stream to test your entire setup. This allows you to check for potential issues without an audience and make necessary adjustments.

- Check for Latency: Latency can be an issue if you're interacting with your audience in real-time. Test the latency during your private stream and adjust settings to minimize delays.

- Simulate Real Conditions: Test your stream under the same conditions as your actual live stream. Use the same internet connection, equipment, and streaming software to ensure that your test results are accurate.

8. Consider a Dedicated Streaming Setup

IF YOU'RE SERIOUS ABOUT live streaming, investing in a dedicated streaming setup can significantly reduce technical issues.
- Use a Streaming PC: A dedicated streaming PC, separate from your main computer, can handle the resource-heavy task of streaming. This reduces the strain on your primary computer and improves overall stability.

- Invest in a Capture Card: If you're streaming from a console or using a high-quality camera, a capture card can provide a stable, high-quality feed to your streaming software.

- Upgrade Your Internet Plan: If your current internet plan struggles to handle live streaming, consider upgrading to a plan with higher upload speeds and more reliable service.

Conclusion

LIVE STREAMING IS AN incredible way to connect with your audience in real-time, but technical glitches can quickly derail even the best-planned streams. By preparing your equipment, optimizing your setup, and having a plan in place to address potential issues, you can minimize disruptions and deliver a seamless live streaming experience. Remember, the key to a successful live stream is preparation, so take the time to test, troubleshoot, and optimize every aspect of your setup before going live. With these hacks, you'll be well on your way to glitch-free streaming and a more professional online presence.

SEO for Musicians: Boosting Website Visibility and Optimizing for Search Engines

In today's digital landscape, having a strong online presence is crucial for musicians. While social media and streaming platforms are essential, your website is the central hub where fans, industry professionals, and potential collaborators can learn more about you and your music. However, having a website isn't enough—you need to make sure it's discoverable. That's where Search Engine Optimization (SEO) comes in. Optimizing your website for search engines can significantly boost your visibility, driving more traffic and helping you reach a broader audience.

Why SEO Matters for Musicians

SEO IS THE PRACTICE of optimizing your website to rank higher in search engine results. When someone searches for a musician or music-related content, you want your site to appear at the top of the results. Higher rankings lead to more clicks, more engagement, and ultimately, more fans. With millions of websites competing for attention, effective SEO can make the difference between being discovered or overlooked.

Key SEO Strategies for Musicians

1. KEYWORD RESEARCH and Optimization
   - Understand Your Audience: Start by identifying the keywords your audience is using to search for music or artists like you. These could include your genre, similar artists, song titles, or even specific events.

- Incorporate Keywords: Use these keywords strategically throughout your website, including in your page titles, meta descriptions, headings, and content. For example, if you're a pop artist, phrases like "pop music artist," "new pop songs," or "indie pop musician" should be integrated naturally into your website text.

2. Optimize Your Website Content

- Create Quality Content: Regularly update your website with fresh content such as blog posts, news updates, tour dates, and new releases. Search engines favor websites that are consistently updated.

- Use Descriptive Text: For every page on your site, use descriptive text that clearly explains who you are and what you offer. Avoid generic language; be specific about your music, your brand, and what makes you unique.

- Optimize Media: Include alt text for images and videos, which helps search engines understand what the media is about. For example, if you post a picture from your latest gig, the alt text could be "Live performance by [Your Name] at [Venue]."

3. Improve Site Structure and Navigation

- User-Friendly Design: Ensure your website is easy to navigate. A well-organized site with clear menus helps both users and search engines find what they're looking for. Include sections for your bio, discography, tour dates, blog, and contact information.

- Internal Linking: Use internal links to connect your content. For example, if you write a blog post about your new album, link to the album's purchase or streaming page. This not only improves navigation but also helps search engines index your site more effectively.

4. Mobile Optimization

- Responsive Design: More than half of all web traffic comes from mobile devices, so it's crucial that your website is mobile-friendly. A responsive design ensures that your site looks and functions well on all devices, which is a factor search engines consider when ranking websites.

- Fast Loading Times: Optimize your website's loading speed by compressing images, reducing the use of heavy scripts, and using a reliable hosting service. Slow websites frustrate users and are penalized by search engines.

5. Build Backlinks

- Get Featured: Backlinks are links from other websites to yours, and they are a key factor in SEO. Reach out to music blogs, online magazines, and influencers to feature your music and link back to your site. Each backlink signals to search engines that your site is trustworthy and authoritative.

- Collaborate with Other Artists: Guest blog on another musician's site or collaborate on a project that links to your website. These collaborations can create valuable backlinks and introduce you to new audiences.

6. Leverage Social Media

- Promote Your Website: Use your social media platforms to drive traffic to your website. Share links to new blog posts, upcoming shows, or your latest music video. The more traffic you generate from social media, the better your SEO performance.

- Consistent Branding: Ensure that your social media profiles link back to your website and maintain consistent branding across all platforms. This builds brand recognition and improves your online presence.

7. Utilize Local SEO

- Optimize for Local Searches: If you perform live regularly or have a strong local following, optimizing for local SEO is essential. Include your location in your keywords and content, such as "Los Angeles indie musician" or "Nashville live music."

- Google My Business: Create a Google My Business profile to improve your visibility in local searches. This can help you appear in Google's local search results and on Google Maps, making it easier for fans to find your live shows or local events.

8. Monitor and Analyze Your Performance

- Use Analytics Tools: Tools like Google Analytics and Google Search Console provide insights into how visitors find and interact with your website. Track metrics like organic traffic, bounce rate, and keyword rankings to understand what's working and what needs improvement.

- Adjust Your Strategy: SEO is an ongoing process. Regularly review your analytics data to identify areas for improvement and adjust your strategy accordingly. Stay up-to-date with SEO trends and algorithm changes to maintain and improve your search engine rankings.

Conclusion

SEO IS A POWERFUL TOOL for musicians who want to boost their website visibility and reach a broader audience. By implementing these strategies, you can ensure that your site is not only user-friendly but also optimized for search engines. Remember, SEO is not a one-time task—it requires ongoing effort and adaptation to stay ahead of the competition. However, the payoff is worth it: increased traffic, more engaged fans, and greater opportunities to grow your music career.

Maintaining Music Gear 101: Troubleshooting Common Instrument Issues

For musicians, instruments are not just tools; they are extensions of creativity and expression. Keeping your gear in top shape is crucial for ensuring that your performance is always at its best. However, like any piece of equipment, instruments can develop issues over time. Understanding how to troubleshoot and maintain your gear can save you time, money, and frustration. Here's a *"Maintaining Music Gear"* guide to help you keep your instruments in peak condition.

1. Stringed Instruments (Guitars, Basses, Violins, etc.)

COMMON ISSUES:
- Buzzing Strings: Often caused by low action or uneven frets.
- Out-of-Tune Strings: Can result from old strings, improper tuning, or a faulty tuning mechanism.
- Dead Spots: Areas on the fretboard where notes don't resonate well.

Troubleshooting Tips:
- Adjust the Truss Rod: If your neck is too straight or bowed, it can cause buzzing. A small truss rod adjustment can help, but if you're unsure, seek a professional.
- Check and Replace Strings: Old or dirty strings can lose tone and tuning stability. Regularly replacing them will keep your sound fresh.
- Inspect Frets: Uneven frets can cause buzzing. Minor issues can be fixed with a fret file, but severe cases may require a professional setup.

2. Keyboards and Synthesizers

COMMON ISSUES:
- Sticky Keys: Keys that don't return to their original position after being pressed.
- Distorted Sound: Unwanted noise or distortion when playing.
- Unresponsive Controls: Knobs or buttons that don't respond correctly.

Troubleshooting Tips:
- Clean the Keys: Dust and debris can cause sticky keys. Carefully cleaning around the keys with a soft cloth and mild cleaner can help.
- Check Connections: Distorted sound can often be traced back to loose or faulty cables. Ensure all connections are secure and cables are in good condition.
- Calibrate or Reset: Some issues with controls can be resolved by recalibrating the instrument or performing a factory reset.

3. Brass and Woodwind Instruments

COMMON ISSUES:
- Sticky Valves or Keys: Valves or keys that don't move smoothly.
- Air Leaks: Loss of air pressure can affect sound quality.
- Cracks or Damage: Physical damage to the instrument body can severely affect performance.

Troubleshooting Tips:
- Oil Valves and Keys: Regularly oiling valves and keys will keep them moving smoothly. Use the correct type of oil for your instrument.
- Inspect Pads and Corks: For woodwinds, check that pads are sealing properly and that corks are not worn. Replace as necessary.
- Check for Cracks: Small cracks can often be repaired with specialized glue or by a professional. Avoid exposing your instrument to extreme temperatures to prevent cracks.

4. Drums and Percussion Instruments

COMMON ISSUES:
- Loose Tension Rods: Can cause heads to go out of tune quickly.
- Damaged Drumheads: Worn or torn drumheads can negatively affect sound.
- Rattling or Buzzing: Unwanted noise from loose hardware or parts.

Troubleshooting Tips:
- Regularly Tune Your Drums: Tighten or loosen tension rods evenly to ensure a balanced sound. Regular tuning will keep your drums sounding their best.
- Replace Worn Heads: Drumheads wear out over time, especially if you play frequently. Replace them regularly to maintain a consistent tone.
- Tighten Hardware: Check and tighten all hardware regularly to prevent rattling and buzzing during play.

5. Amplifiers and Effects Pedals

COMMON ISSUES:
- No Sound or Weak Signal: Can be caused by a faulty cable, connection, or internal component.
- Humming or Buzzing: Electrical interference or grounding issues.
- Non-Responsive Controls: Knobs or switches that don't seem to work.

Troubleshooting Tips:
- Check Your Cables: Faulty cables are a common cause of no sound or weak signal. Swap out cables to diagnose the issue.
- Isolate the Problem: Disconnect everything and add one component at a time to find the source of noise or interference.

- Clean the Pots: If your controls are scratchy or unresponsive, cleaning the potentiometers with contact cleaner can often solve the issue.

Final Thoughts

ROUTINE MAINTENANCE is the key to extending the life of your gear and ensuring it performs at its best. While some issues can be easily fixed at home, don't hesitate to seek professional help for more complex problems. Remember, a well-maintained instrument not only sounds better but also feels better to play, allowing you to focus on what truly matters—making music.

How To Safely Clean an Electric Guitar

Taking care of your electric guitar is crucial not only for maintaining its appearance but also for preserving its sound quality and longevity. Regular cleaning can prevent the buildup of dirt and grime that can affect your guitar's performance. Here's a step-by-step guide on how to safely clean your electric guitar.

1. Gather the Right Tools

BEFORE YOU START, MAKE sure you have the following items:
- Microfiber cloths: Soft and lint-free, these are perfect for cleaning the guitar without scratching it.
- Guitar polish: Specifically formulated for guitars, this helps maintain the finish without causing damage.
- String cleaner/lubricant: To clean and protect your strings.
- Soft bristle brush: For hard-to-reach areas like between pickups.
- Cotton swabs: Useful for small crevices.
- Isopropyl alcohol: For cleaning metal parts like strings (optional).

2. Remove the Strings

BEFORE CLEANING, IT'S best to remove the strings. This gives you full access to the fretboard and body.
- Loosen the strings using the tuning pegs and then carefully unwind them from the bridge and tuners.
- Dispose of the old strings if you plan to replace them, or set them aside if you'll reuse them.

3. Clean the Fretboard

THE FRETBOARD CAN ACCUMULATE dirt and oils from your fingers over time.

- Wipe down the fretboard with a dry microfiber cloth to remove loose debris.

- Use a slightly dampened cloth with water or a specialized fretboard cleaner if it's particularly dirty. Be sure not to over-wet the cloth, as excess moisture can damage the wood.

- For unfinished fretboards (like rosewood or ebony), consider using a small amount of fretboard conditioner or lemon oil. Apply it sparingly with a clean cloth, and let it sit for a few minutes before wiping off the excess.

4. Clean the Body

THE BODY OF YOUR GUITAR needs special care to maintain its shine.

- Wipe the body with a dry microfiber cloth to remove dust and fingerprints.

- Apply a small amount of guitar polish to the cloth, not directly onto the guitar, and gently buff the surface. Avoid using household cleaners or abrasive products, as they can damage the finish.

- Pay attention to the pickguard and around the pickups. Use a soft bristle brush to remove dirt from around the edges.

5. Clean the Hardware

METAL PARTS LIKE THE bridge, tuners, and pickups can tarnish over time.

- Wipe down the hardware with a dry cloth. If there's any stubborn grime, use a dampened cloth with isopropyl alcohol, but be careful not to get it on the guitar's finish.

- Use a cotton swab to clean tight spaces around the hardware.

- For tarnished metal, a small amount of metal polish can be used on a cloth, but avoid contact with the guitar's finish.

6. Clean the Strings (If Reusing)

IF YOU'RE NOT REPLACING the strings, cleaning them can extend their lifespan.

- Use a string cleaner or lubricant to remove oils and dirt from the strings.

- Wipe the strings with a clean cloth after applying the cleaner, ensuring they are dry and free of residue.

7. Reassemble and Tune Up

ONCE EVERYTHING IS clean, it's time to put the strings back on.

- Restring the guitar, starting with the low E string and working your way to the high E string.

- Tune the guitar to your desired pitch.

- Give the guitar a final wipe down to remove any fingerprints or smudges from the cleaning process.

Final Tips

- REGULAR CLEANING: Make it a habit to wipe down your guitar after each use to prevent grime buildup.

- Store properly: Keep your guitar in its case when not in use to protect it from dust and humidity.

- Handle with care: Always use soft cloths and gentle products designed for guitars to avoid damaging your instrument.

By following these steps, you can keep your electric guitar looking great and performing at its best for years to come. Happy playing!

Proven Techniques for Optimizing Website Efficiency

How to begin Optimizing Website Efficiency: Proven Strategies for Webmasters

IN TODAY'S DIGITAL age, where attention spans are short and competition is fierce, having a fast and high-performing website is crucial to success. Webmasters play a pivotal role in ensuring that websites not only look great but also load quickly. Optimizing website efficiency and speed is a multifaceted task that requires a combination of technical know-how and best practices. In this comprehensive guide, we will dive into the strategies and techniques that webmasters can implement to supercharge the speed and performance of their websites.

Understanding the Importance of Website Speed

WEBSITE SPEED IS NOT just a convenience for users; it directly impacts metrics such as user experience, bounce rates, and even search engine rankings. Studies have shown that visitors tend to abandon a website if it takes more than a few seconds to load, highlighting the critical role that speed plays in retaining visitors and driving conversions.

Diagnosing Performance Issues

BEFORE DIVING INTO optimization strategies, it's essential to identify the root causes of slow performance. Common culprits include large image files, excessive plugins, inefficient code, and server-related issues. By conducting a thorough audit using tools like Google

PageSpeed Insights or GTmetrix, webmasters can pinpoint areas that need improvement.

Proven Strategies for Optimization

1. OPTIMIZE IMAGES

Images are often the heaviest elements on a webpage. By compressing images without compromising quality, leveraging next-gen formats like WebP, and lazy loading images below the fold, webmasters can significantly reduce loading times.

2. MINIFY CSS AND JAVASCRIPT

Minification involves removing unnecessary characters from code without altering its functionality. This simple yet effective technique reduces file sizes, leading to faster loading speeds.

3. Utilize Browser Caching

Enabling browser caching instructs visitors' browsers to store static assets locally, reducing the need to re-download content on subsequent visits. Implementing optimal caching policies can drastically improve website performance.

4. Content Delivery Network (CDN)

CDNs distribute website content across multiple servers worldwide, enabling faster delivery based on users' geographic locations. By leveraging a CDN, webmasters can reduce latency and enhance overall site performance.

5. Optimize Server Performance

Choosing a reliable hosting provider, configuring server settings for optimal performance, and implementing server-side caching mechanisms are essential steps to ensure that the backend infrastructure supports fast loading times.

6. Monitor Performance Metrics

Regularly monitoring performance metrics such as page load time, time to first byte (TTFB), and resource loading sequences can provide insights into the effectiveness of optimization efforts. Tools like Google Analytics and New Relic are invaluable for tracking and analyzing performance data.

Final Thoughts

IN THE COMPETITIVE online landscape, website speed can be a game-changer. By prioritizing optimization strategies and staying abreast of the latest industry trends, webmasters can elevate their websites to new levels of speed and performance. Remember, a fast website not only delights users but also boosts conversions and improves search engine visibility.

Optimizing website performance is an ongoing journey, but with the right tools and techniques at your disposal, you can propel your website to success in the digital realm.

Implement these strategies today and watch your website soar to new heights of speed and performance!

Stay tuned for more insightful tips and tricks for webmasters as we continue to explore the dynamic world of website optimization. Remember, speed matters in the digital race!

Let's revolutionize your website's performance and speed together! Start optimizing today and witness the transformation firsthand. Your users will thank you, and search engines will reward you. Happy optimizing!

Professional Tips for Home Studio Success

In the digital age of music production, the luxury of recording in the comfort of your own home has become increasingly popular among musicians and creators. Whether you're a seasoned musician looking to add tracks to your portfolio or an aspiring artist delving into the world of home recording, mastering the art of recording at home is essential. In this guide "Professional Tips for Home Studio Success", we will explore professional tips and techniques to elevate your home studio recordings from amateur to industry-standard quality.

Setting Up Your Home Studio

THE FOUNDATION OF A successful recording starts with a properly set up home studio. Find a quiet and acoustically treated space where outside noise is minimal. Invest in quality studio monitors, microphones, and an audio interface to ensure pristine sound capture. Organize your studio layout for optimal workflow, keeping essential equipment within reach.

Understanding Room Acoustics

ACOUSTIC TREATMENT plays a crucial role in achieving professional-sounding recordings. Consider acoustic panels, bass traps, and diffusers to minimize unwanted reflections, reverberations, and standing waves. Experiment with microphone placement to find the sweet spot in your room that enhances the sound quality of your recordings.

Embracing the Basics of Recording

WHEN IT COMES TO RECORDING at home, attention to detail is key. Ensure proper gain staging to prevent unwanted distortion and noise. Experiment with microphone techniques such as close miking, mid-side recording, and room miking to capture different sonic textures. Don't underestimate the power of a well-executed performance; the emotion and energy you convey in your recordings are just as important as technical proficiency.

Leveraging Digital Audio Workstations (DAWs)

CHOOSE A DAW THAT SUITS your workflow and learn its ins and outs. Familiarize yourself with editing tools, plugins, and virtual instruments to enhance the sonic palette of your recordings. Explore the world of mixing and mastering to polish your tracks and elevate them to a professional standard. Remember, practice makes perfect, so keep honing your skills to unleash your creative potential.

Experimenting with Production Techniques

BREAK FREE FROM THE constraints of traditional recording techniques and experiment with unconventional approaches. Incorporate sampling, looping, and creative effects to add depth and character to your recordings. Collaboration with other musicians, producers, and artists can bring fresh perspectives and innovative ideas to your music.

Cultivating Your Unique Sound

WHILE MASTERING HOME recording techniques involves technical proficiency, it is also about finding your unique voice as a creator. Embrace imperfections, take risks, and trust your instincts. Your home studio is a playground for creativity, where experimentation and exploration lead to artistic growth.

Conclusion

MASTERING HOME RECORDING techniques is a rewarding journey that requires dedication, patience, and a willingness to push boundaries. By following these professional tips and techniques, you can unlock the full potential of your home studio and create music that resonates with listeners. Remember, the art of recording at home is not just about capturing sound; it's about capturing emotions, stories, and moments in time. So, fire up your studio, unleash your creativity, and embark on a musical adventure like never before.

Happy recording!

Understanding MIDI Technology: A Beginner's Guide

Have you ever listened to a piece of music and wondered how it all comes together seamlessly? Have you ever been curious about the magic that happens behind the scenes in music production? If you're a budding music enthusiast eager to understand the intricacies of music creation, then delving into the realm of MIDI technology might just be the key to unlocking a whole new world of possibilities.

The Dawn of MIDI

MIDI, SHORT FOR MUSICAL Instrument Digital Interface, serves as the backbone of modern music production. This universal language allows electronic musical instruments, computers, and other devices to communicate and synchronize with each other. Originally introduced in the early 1980s, MIDI revolutionized the way music is created, recorded, and produced.

Understanding the Basics

AT ITS CORE, MIDI IS not sound itself, but rather a set of instructions that dictate how sounds are produced. These instructions include note values, pitch, velocity, modulation, and more. Think of MIDI as the conductor of an orchestra, directing each instrument on what to play, when to play it, and how it should be played.

MIDI in Music Production

IN THE REALM OF MUSIC production, MIDI opens up a world of limitless possibilities. Whether you're composing your own music, arranging existing pieces, or experimenting with different sounds, MIDI empowers you to unleash your creativity without the constraints of traditional instruments.

Getting Started with MIDI

TO EMBARK ON YOUR MIDI journey, you'll need a MIDI controller such as a keyboard or pad controller, a digital audio workstation (DAW) software, and a basic understanding of music theory. MIDI controllers act as the bridge between your musical ideas and the digital realm, allowing you to input notes, adjust parameters, and create intricate melodies with ease.

The Future of MIDI

AS TECHNOLOGY CONTINUES to advance, so does the landscape of MIDI technology. With the rise of virtual instruments, plugins, and innovative MIDI-enabled devices, the possibilities for music creation are evolving at a rapid pace. Whether you're a seasoned producer or a beginner exploring the world of music, MIDI remains a fundamental tool in shaping the future of music production.

Conclusion

IF YOU'RE READY TO embark on a musical journey filled with creativity, innovation, and boundless opportunities, then diving into the world of MIDI technology is a step in the right direction. From unraveling the intricacies of MIDI messages to exploring the endless possibilities of music production, this universal language holds the key to unlocking your full musical potential.

So, embrace the mystery, embrace the magic, and embark on your very own novice's journey into the captivating world of MIDI technology!

Remember, in the world of music production, the only limit is your imagination. Let MIDI be your guide to limitless musical creativity and innovation.

Unlocking the Perfect Sound: Troubleshooting Audio Quality Issues

Achieving perfect sound quality is the goal of every music producer, sound engineer, and performer. Whether you're recording in a studio or performing live, audio quality can make or break your work. But even with the best equipment, issues can arise. Here's a guide to troubleshooting audio quality issues and improving sound quality during recording sessions and live performances.

1. Identify the Source of the Problem

BEFORE YOU CAN FIX an audio issue, you need to identify the source. Audio problems can stem from various places—your equipment, environment, or even your settings.

- Check Your Signal Chain: Start by inspecting every part of your signal chain, from the microphone or instrument to the final output. Ensure that all cables are securely connected and that there are no loose connections. A faulty cable or connection is often the culprit behind unwanted noise or dropouts.

- Test Your Gear Individually: If you're not sure where the problem lies, test each piece of equipment individually. This helps isolate the issue, whether it's a specific microphone, cable, or interface.

- Environmental Factors: Sometimes, the environment can introduce noise into your recordings. Background noise, electrical interference, and even the acoustics of your room can affect sound quality. Identifying and mitigating these factors can significantly improve your recordings.

2. Reduce Background Noise

UNWANTED BACKGROUND noise can be a significant issue during both recording and live performances. Reducing noise at the source is always the best approach.

- Use Noise Gates: A noise gate can help eliminate low-level background noise by cutting off the sound when it falls below a certain threshold. This is especially useful in live performances where ambient noise can be unpredictable.

- Choose the Right Microphone: Different microphones pick up sound differently. For example, cardioid microphones are great for reducing background noise because they primarily pick up sound from the front. Condenser microphones, while sensitive, can pick up more background noise, so be mindful of your environment when using them.

- Soundproofing and Acoustic Treatment: In a recording environment, soundproofing your room and adding acoustic treatment can drastically reduce external noise and improve sound quality. Foam panels, bass traps, and diffusers can help control reflections and echoes.

3. Avoid Distortion

DISTORTION CAN RUIN an otherwise perfect recording or live performance. It usually occurs when your input levels are too high, causing the sound to clip.

- Monitor Input Levels: Always keep an eye on your input levels to ensure they stay within a safe range. Most DAWs and mixing consoles have meters that indicate when your signal is peaking. Aim to keep your levels in the green, avoiding the red zone where clipping occurs.

- Use a Limiter: A limiter can prevent distortion by capping your signal's peak level. This is particularly useful during live performances, where unexpected volume spikes can lead to distortion.

- Adjust Gain Staging: Proper gain staging—setting the right levels at each point in your signal chain—ensures that your signal is strong enough without being too hot. Start by setting the gain on your microphone or instrument, then adjust the levels on your preamp, interface, and DAW accordingly.

4. Manage Frequency Balance

A WELL-BALANCED MIX is crucial for clarity and impact. Issues with frequency balance can lead to muddy or harsh sound, making your audio less pleasing to the ear.

- EQ Your Tracks: Use an equalizer (EQ) to carve out space for each instrument in the mix. For example, cutting unnecessary low frequencies from vocals can prevent them from clashing with the bass or kick drum. Similarly, reducing harsh high frequencies can make your mix sound smoother.

- Use Reference Tracks: Comparing your mix to a professionally produced track in a similar genre can help you identify frequency imbalances. Adjust your EQ until your mix sounds balanced and comparable to the reference.

- Watch Out for Overlapping Frequencies: Instruments that occupy the same frequency range can cause a cluttered mix. Use EQ to reduce overlapping frequencies and give each element its own space.

5. Optimize Your Recording Environment

YOUR RECORDING ENVIRONMENT plays a significant role in sound quality. Poor acoustics can lead to unwanted reflections, reverb, and phase issues.

- Position Your Microphone Carefully: The placement of your microphone in the room can affect the sound. Experiment with different positions to find the spot with the least amount of unwanted reflections or reverb. Close miking can also reduce the impact of room acoustics.

- Use Acoustic Treatment: As mentioned earlier, acoustic treatment helps control the sound in your recording space. In addition to foam panels and bass traps, consider using diffusers to scatter sound waves and prevent harsh reflections.

- Record in a Quiet Space: The quieter your recording space, the better. Turn off fans, air conditioners, and other noise sources, and choose a room away from busy streets or noisy neighbors.

6. Enhance Clarity with Compression

COMPRESSION IS A POWERFUL tool for controlling dynamics and enhancing the clarity of your recordings.

- Set Your Threshold and Ratio Correctly: The threshold determines when the compressor kicks in, while the ratio controls how much compression is applied. Start with a gentle ratio (e.g., 2:1) and adjust the threshold until the dynamics are controlled without sounding squashed.

- Use Parallel Compression: Parallel compression, also known as New York compression, involves blending a heavily compressed version of a track with the original signal. This technique can add punch and clarity without sacrificing dynamics.

- Avoid Over-Compression: While compression is useful, over-compressing can make your mix sound lifeless and flat. Use it sparingly, focusing on enhancing clarity and consistency rather than eliminating all dynamic range.

7. Test and Adjust in Real-Time

IN LIVE PERFORMANCES, sound quality can be affected by the acoustics of the venue, the PA system, and even the audience. Testing and adjusting in real-time is essential.

- Perform Sound Checks: Always conduct a thorough sound check before your performance. Test each microphone, instrument, and monitor to ensure everything sounds clear and balanced. Use this time to identify any potential issues and address them before the show starts.

- Use In-Ear Monitors: In-ear monitors (IEMs) allow you to hear yourself clearly during a performance, helping you identify any sound issues as they arise. IEMs also reduce the risk of feedback, which can be a common problem with traditional stage monitors.

- Have a Backup Plan: Always have backup equipment on hand in case something goes wrong during a performance. Extra cables, microphones, and even a secondary audio interface can save the day if issues arise.

Conclusion

ACHIEVING PERFECT SOUND quality is a combination of preparation, attention to detail, and quick thinking. By identifying and addressing audio issues at their source, managing your recording environment, and using the right tools, you can ensure that your recordings and live performances sound their best. Remember, great sound quality isn't just about having the best gear—it's about knowing how to use it effectively to create the best possible audio experience.

Mastering Your Mix: Common Mixing Problems and Solutions

Mixing is an art that can elevate a track from good to great, but it comes with its own set of challenges. Even experienced producers can run into issues that make a mix sound muddy, harsh, or unbalanced. Whether you're a beginner or a seasoned pro, understanding common mixing problems and how to solve them is crucial to mastering your mix. Here's a guide to help you tackle some of the most frequent mixing challenges.

1. Muddy Mixes

A MUDDY MIX LACKS CLARITY, making it difficult to distinguish between different instruments and sounds. This problem is often caused by too many low frequencies overlapping, particularly in the bass and lower midrange.

- Solution: EQ the Low-End Carefully
- High-Pass Filter: Apply a high-pass filter to instruments that don't need low frequencies, such as vocals, guitars, and even some synths. This helps clear up space for the bass and kick drum.
- Cut Low-Mid Frequencies: Mud often resides in the 200-500 Hz range. Gently cut these frequencies on tracks that contribute to the muddiness, but be careful not to overdo it and thin out your mix.
- Use Sidechain Compression: Sidechain the bass to the kick drum to prevent them from clashing and create a cleaner low end.

2. Harsh Highs

HARSHNESS IN THE HIGH frequencies can make a mix sound unpleasant and fatiguing to listen to. This often happens when instruments or vocals are too bright or when there's too much sibilance in the vocals.

- Solution: Tame the High Frequencies
- Use a De-Esser: A de-esser targets and reduces sibilance in vocal tracks, making them smoother and less harsh. Adjust the threshold and frequency range until the sibilance is under control.
- EQ Cuts: Identify the harsh frequencies, usually between 2 kHz and 10 kHz, and apply a gentle cut. Be subtle—cutting too much can dull the track.
- Saturation: Adding a touch of saturation can help smooth out harsh highs by adding warmth and rounding off the edges of the sound.

3. Weak Vocals

VOCALS ARE OFTEN THE focal point of a mix, and if they sound weak or buried, it can detract from the overall impact of the track.

- Solution: Make Vocals Stand Out
- Compression: Use compression to control the dynamics of the vocal, ensuring that softer parts are audible and louder parts aren't overwhelming. A ratio of 3:1 or 4:1 is a good starting point.
- EQ Boosts: Boost the presence range around 3 kHz to 6 kHz to help the vocals cut through the mix. If needed, add some air by boosting around 10 kHz to 12 kHz.
- Reverb and Delay: Apply reverb or delay to add depth to the vocals, but be careful not to overdo it. Too much reverb can push the vocals back in the mix. Instead, use a subtle, short reverb or a slap-back delay to keep the vocals forward.

4. Overcrowded Mix

WHEN TOO MANY ELEMENTS compete for space in the mix, it can sound cluttered and chaotic, making it hard for the listener to focus on any one part.

- Solution: Create Space with Panning and EQ

- Panning: Spread out the elements across the stereo field. Pan instruments like guitars, keyboards, and backing vocals to the left or right, leaving the center for the kick, bass, and lead vocals.

- EQ Subtractive Mixing: Use EQ to carve out space for each element. For instance, if two instruments are clashing in the same frequency range, cut the clashing frequencies on one instrument and boost them slightly on the other.

- Use Reverb Wisely: Apply reverb to create a sense of space, but don't overuse it. Too much reverb can make a mix sound washy and undefined.

5. Lack of Depth

A MIX THAT LACKS DEPTH can sound flat and one-dimensional. This often happens when all the elements are placed at the same volume and don't have enough contrast.

- Solution: Add Depth with Volume Automation and Effects

- Volume Automation: Use automation to bring certain elements forward during key moments and push others back. This creates a dynamic and engaging mix.

- Reverb and Delay: Apply reverb and delay to create a sense of space and depth. Use shorter, more subtle reverb on elements you want closer to the listener, and longer, more pronounced reverb on elements you want to push back.

- Layering: Layer sounds to create more texture and depth. For example, layer a dry signal with a reverb-drenched version of the same signal to add dimension.

6. Over-Compression

OVER-COMPRESSION CAN lead to a lifeless, squashed mix that lacks dynamics and feels flat. While compression is a valuable tool, it's important to use it judiciously.
- Solution: Use Compression Sparingly
- Set Proper Threshold and Ratio: Start with a low ratio (2:1 or 3:1) and set the threshold so that the compressor only engages when necessary. This preserves the natural dynamics of the track.
- Parallel Compression: Instead of compressing the entire signal, use parallel compression. Blend the compressed signal with the uncompressed signal to retain the punch and dynamics.
- Watch the Attack and Release Times: Adjust the attack and release times to suit the material. A slow attack allows transients to pass through, maintaining the punch, while a fast release can help keep the track lively.

7. Stereo Imbalance

A MIX WITH STEREO IMBALANCE can sound lopsided or off-center, making it less enjoyable to listen to. This often happens when elements are panned too hard or unevenly distributed across the stereo field.
- Solution: Balance the Stereo Field
- Check Your Panning: Ensure that your elements are evenly distributed across the stereo field. Avoid panning too many elements hard left or right; instead, find a balance that feels natural.

- Use Mid/Side Processing: Mid/Side processing allows you to control the center (mid) and sides of your mix independently. This can help you correct any imbalance and create a more cohesive stereo image.
- Mono Compatibility: Regularly check your mix in mono to ensure that it translates well. Some stereo effects can cause phase issues when collapsed to mono, so it's important to test this during the mixing process.

8. Lack of Energy

A MIX THAT LACKS ENERGY can sound dull and uninspiring. This often happens when the mix doesn't have enough contrast or excitement, causing it to feel flat.
- Solution: Add Energy with Contrast and Dynamics
- Automation: Use automation to create dynamic shifts in your mix. Gradual buildups, drops, and changes in volume can add excitement and keep the listener engaged.
- Enhance Transients: Use transient shapers or compression with a slow attack to enhance the transients of drums and percussive elements, giving them more punch and energy.
- Layer Percussion: Adding layers of percussion, such as claps, shakers, or cymbals, can inject energy into a mix, especially during key sections like the chorus or drop.

Conclusion

MIXING IS A COMPLEX and creative process, but it doesn't have to be overwhelming. By understanding and addressing these common mixing problems, you can achieve a polished and professional sound. Remember, mixing is about making decisions that serve the song, so trust your ears, experiment, and don't be afraid to make bold choices. With practice and attention to detail, you can master your mix and bring your music to life.

Choosing the Right DAW for Music Production

Music production is a craft that demands dedication, creativity, and, of course, the right tools. When diving into the world of music production, one of the fundamental choices you'll face is selecting the right Digital Audio Workstation (DAW) to bring your musical visions to life. With an overwhelming array of options available, from industry standards to beginner-friendly software, it's crucial in choosing the right DAW that it not only meets your needs but also nurtures your growth as an aspiring music producer.

Understanding DAWs: The Building Blocks of Your Musical Journey

DIGITAL AUDIO WORKSTATIONS serve as the backbone of your music production process, offering a platform where you can create, edit, arrange, and mix sound recordings with precision and efficiency. Each DAW comes with its unique features, interface, and workflow, catering to different levels of expertise and musical genres. For beginners, the challenge lies in finding a DAW that strikes a balance between user-friendliness and powerful capabilities.

The Top Contenders: Exploring DAWs for Beginners

1. GARAGEBAND (MAC)

AS AN ENTRY-LEVEL DAW exclusive to Mac users, GarageBand offers a seamless introduction to music production. With its intuitive interface, pre-installed loops, and virtual instruments, GarageBand allows beginners to start creating music without a steep learning curve. While limited in advanced features compared to other software, GarageBand provides a solid foundation for honing your production skills.

2. FL Studio

FL Studio, known for its user-friendly interface and comprehensive feature set, is a popular choice among beginners and professionals alike. Offering a wide range of built-in plugins, virtual instruments, and a step sequencer, FL Studio empowers users to compose, mix, and master tracks with ease. Its pattern-based workflow simplifies the music creation process, making it an attractive option for those new to music production.

3. Ableton Live

Ableton Live stands out for its versatility in both studio production and live performances, making it a favorite among electronic music producers. With its innovative Session View and flexible arrangement options, Ableton Live encourages experimentation and improvisation in music creation. While its interface may seem daunting at first, the wealth of tutorials and online resources available can aid beginners in mastering this powerful DAW.

Choosing the Right DAW: A Personalized Decision

WHEN SELECTING A DAW as a beginner, it's essential to consider your musical goals, preferred genre, and workflow preferences. While each DAW has its strengths and limitations, the ideal software for you is one that aligns with your creative vision and enhances your productivity. Take the time to explore different options, experiment with their features, and choose a DAW that resonates with your artistic aspirations.

Conclusion

In the realm of music production, the choice of DAW can significantly impact your creative journey. As a beginner, investing time and effort in selecting the right software can set the stage for your growth and development as a music producer. Whether you opt for the simplicity of GarageBand, the versatility of FL Studio, or the innovation of Ableton Live, remember that your DAW is not just a tool but a companion in your musical endeavors. Embrace the learning process, unleash your creativity, and let your chosen DAW be the canvas on which your musical masterpieces unfold.

Unveil the perfect DAW that resonates with your passion for music and watch as your creative aspirations take flight. Let your music speak volumes, guided by the harmony between your talent and the ideal music production software.

Unveiling the Perfect DAW: A Beginner's Guide to Choosing the Ideal Music Production Software serves as your gateway to the world of music production, offering insights, recommendations, and inspiration to fuel your creative pursuits. Explore the possibilities, harness your creativity, and embark on a musical journey like no other with the perfect DAW by your side.

Setting Up Your FL Studio for Vocal Recording Success

In the world of music production, the tools at your disposal play a crucial role in shaping the quality of your output. Aspiring producers often wonder if it's possible to achieve professional-grade results without owning traditional recording equipment. This dilemma is particularly common among those who rely solely on software like FL Studio to record and mix vocals, using downloaded beats as their backdrop. Can one truly master the art of producing without the physical equipment typically associated with the trade? Let's delve into this topic and uncover the essentials for creating top-notch vocal recordings and mixes using FL Studio for vocal recording success.

Why Equipment Matters in Music Production

BEFORE WE DIVE INTO the specifics of recording vocals and mixing tracks, let's address the importance of the equipment used in the music production process. While software like FL Studio provides a powerful platform for creating music, the quality of your recordings is not solely dependent on the software itself. Factors such as microphone quality, audio interfaces, and studio monitors significantly impact the overall sound of your production. However, this does not mean that aspiring producers without traditional equipment are doomed to mediocrity. With a strategic approach and a nuanced understanding of digital tools, remarkable results can still be achieved.

Recording Vocals with FL Studio: Making the Most of Limited Resources

IF YOU FIND YOURSELF in a situation where traditional recording equipment is out of reach, fear not. FL Studio boasts a range of features that can help you capture clean and professional vocal recordings. Here's a step-by-step guide to optimizing your vocal recording process within FL Studio:

- **Selecting a Quality Microphone** : While a dedicated studio microphone is optimal, you can still achieve decent results with a high-quality USB microphone. Position the microphone correctly and experiment with different settings to find the best sound for your vocals.

- **Utilizing FL Studio Effects** : Take advantage of FL Studio's built-in effects such as reverb, compression, and EQ to enhance the quality of your vocals. Experiment with these effects to find the right balance for your tracks.

- **Editing and Compiling Takes** : FL Studio offers robust editing tools that allow you to fine-tune your vocal recordings. Take the time to edit out any imperfections and compile multiple takes to create a polished final product.

Mixing Vocals and Beats: Striking the Perfect Balance

ONCE YOU HAVE RECORDED your vocals, the next step is to mix them with your downloaded beats to create a cohesive and professional-sounding track. Here's how you can achieve a balanced mix using FL Studio:

- **Panning and Balancing** : Utilize FL Studio's panning feature to position your vocals and beats in the stereo field. Balance the levels of each element to ensure that they complement each other without overwhelming the mix.

- **Adding Effects and Processing** : Experiment with FL Studio's effects plugins to add depth and character to your vocals and beats. Use EQ to carve out space for each element and compression to control dynamics.

- **Mastering the Final Mix** : Once you are satisfied with the individual elements of your track, use FL Studio's mastering tools to give your mix a final polish. Pay attention to levels, tonal balance, and overall cohesiveness to ensure a professional-quality outcome.

By harnessing the capabilities of FL Studio and mastering the techniques outlined above, aspiring producers can overcome the limitations of not owning traditional recording equipment. While having access to dedicated hardware undoubtedly offers advantages, the digital landscape has expanded the possibilities for creating high-quality music from virtually anywhere.

Remember, it's not about the equipment you own, but rather how you leverage the tools at your disposal to craft exceptional music. With dedication, creativity, and a keen ear, you can elevate your productions to professional standards, even with limited resources.

What If I Regret My Music Production Equipment Purchase?

Investing in music production gear is an exciting step toward pursuing your creative ambitions. However, the thought of changing your mind after making such a significant investment can be daunting. What If I regret my music production equipment purchase? Here's how to navigate this scenario without regret.

1. Reframe Your Perspective

FIRST, IT'S ESSENTIAL to reframe how you view this situation. Buying music production gear doesn't have to be seen as a waste if you change your mind. Instead, consider it as part of your creative exploration. Many hobbies and interests require some level of investment to discover whether they're the right fit for you.

2. Consider Alternative Uses for the Gear

EVEN IF YOU DECIDE that music production isn't your passion, the gear you've purchased likely has other uses:
  - Podcasting or Voiceover Work: Many pieces of music production equipment, like microphones, audio interfaces, and headphones, can be used for podcasting or voiceover projects. These fields are growing in popularity and could open up new creative avenues for you.
  - Content Creation: If you're interested in creating YouTube videos, streaming, or other types of content, your production gear can enhance the quality of your recordings, helping you stand out in a crowded digital space.
  - Learning and Experimentation: Your gear can also be used to learn about audio engineering, mixing, or sound design—skills that are valuable across multiple creative disciplines.

3. Sell or Trade Your Gear

THE MUSIC PRODUCTION community is vast and often full of people looking to buy second-hand gear at a fair price. If you decide to move on, you can:

- Sell Online: Platforms like eBay, Reverb, or specialized music gear marketplaces make it easy to list your equipment. If you take good care of your gear, you can recoup a significant portion of your investment.

- Trade or Swap: Some communities and forums offer opportunities to trade or swap gear with other producers. This could allow you to exchange your equipment for something that aligns more with your current interests.

4. Renting or Leasing Gear in the Future

IF YOU'RE CONCERNED about making another large investment in the future, consider renting or leasing equipment instead of purchasing it outright. This approach allows you to try out different setups and determine what works best for you without a long-term commitment.

5. Gain Valuable Experience

EVEN IF YOU DECIDE not to continue with music production, the experience you've gained is invaluable. You've likely developed skills in areas like audio editing, software navigation, and creative problem-solving, which are transferable to other fields. These skills can be beneficial in various creative and technical professions.

6. Reflect on Your Journey

CHANGING YOUR MIND isn't a failure—it's part of the creative process. Reflect on what you've learned about yourself, your interests, and your creative goals. This self-awareness will guide you toward pursuits that are more fulfilling and aligned with your passions.

7. Keep the Door Open

JUST BECAUSE YOU'VE decided to step away from music production now doesn't mean you can't return to it later. Creative interests often ebb and flow. By keeping your gear or holding onto your newfound skills, you leave the door open to revisit music production when the time feels right.

Conclusion

INVESTING IN MUSIC production gear is a significant step, but changing your mind afterward doesn't have to be a source of regret. Whether you find alternative uses for your equipment, sell it, or apply your skills in new ways, you can turn this experience into a positive one. Remember, every creative journey involves twists and turns—what's important is that you learn and grow from each step along the way.

How to Record Music at Home Without Disturbing Neighbors

Producing music is a deeply rewarding experience, but it can also pose challenges, particularly when you live in close proximity to others. One of the biggest concerns for any home-based music producer is the impact of noise on neighbors. Here's how you can record music at home without disturbing neighbors and continue creating music without upsetting those around you.

1. Soundproof Your Space

SOUNDPROOFING IS THE most effective way to minimize noise
leakage. Here's how you can do it:
    - Acoustic Panels: Installing acoustic panels on the walls of your
studio can absorb sound, reducing the amount that escapes. These
panels are designed to target specific frequencies, helping to keep your
bass and treble levels contained.
    - Sealing Gaps: Doors, windows, and other gaps are notorious for
letting sound escape. Weather stripping and door sweeps can help seal
these gaps, while heavy curtains or soundproof window inserts can
block sound leakage from windows.
    - Floating Floor: If you're serious about soundproofing, consider
installing a floating floor. This is a floor that sits on a layer of padding,
isolating it from the structural floor and preventing vibrations from
traveling through the building.

2. Use Headphones

HEADPHONES ARE AN INVALUABLE tool for producers who
need to keep noise levels down. High-quality studio headphones allow
you to hear every detail of your mix without disturbing others.
Closed-back headphones, in particular, are great for preventing sound
leakage.

3. Consider Your Timing

EVEN IF YOU'RE WELL soundproofed, consider the timing of your
sessions. Producing music during hours when your neighbors are less
likely to be home or awake can prevent potential conflicts.

4. Adjust Your Monitor Levels

IT'S EASY TO GET CARRIED away with the volume when you're in the zone, but constantly cranking up your monitors can lead to issues. Keep your monitor levels reasonable, and try to keep bass levels low as these frequencies tend to travel further.

5. Communicate with Your Neighbors

OPEN COMMUNICATION is key. Let your neighbors know that you produce music and ask if they have any concerns about noise. Sometimes, just being considerate and checking in can go a long way in preventing complaints. They may appreciate your efforts to minimize disruption, and you can establish a more understanding relationship.

6. Invest in Isolation Pads

ISOLATION PADS ARE a small investment with big returns. These pads sit underneath your monitors or speakers and help to reduce vibrations that can travel through your desk or floor, minimizing the noise your neighbors hear.

7. Use Software Solutions

IF PHYSICAL SOUNDPROOFING isn't an option, consider using software solutions that allow you to mix and produce at lower volumes. Tools like Sonarworks Reference can help you achieve accurate mixes even at low levels, reducing the need to blast your speakers.

Conclusion

PRODUCING MUSIC AT home without disturbing your neighbors is not only possible but can also be relatively straightforward with the right approach. By investing in soundproofing, using headphones, managing your noise levels, and maintaining good communication, you can create music peacefully and productively. Remember, a little consideration goes a long way in maintaining harmony—not just in your tracks, but in your community as well.

Website Loading Woes: Speed Optimization for Musicians

In today's fast-paced digital world, your website is often the first impression you make on potential fans, collaborators, and industry professionals. A slow-loading site can turn visitors away before they even get a chance to hear your music or learn about your upcoming shows. Speed optimization for musicians isn't just a technical concern; it's a crucial part of building and maintaining an effective online presence. In this post, we'll explore practical tips to optimize your website's loading times and ensure a smooth, fast experience for your visitors.

1. Choose the Right Hosting Provider

YOUR WEBSITE'S PERFORMANCE starts with your hosting provider. A reliable and fast web host is essential for quick loading times.

- Shared vs. Dedicated Hosting: While shared hosting is cheaper, it often results in slower load times due to the number of sites sharing the same server. If you can afford it, consider upgrading to a dedicated hosting plan or a Virtual Private Server (VPS) for better performance.

- Content Delivery Network (CDN): A CDN stores copies of your site's content on servers around the world, delivering it to users from the nearest server. This reduces the distance data has to travel and speeds up loading times for your global audience.

2. Optimize Your Images

IMAGES ARE OFTEN THE largest files on a website, and unoptimized images can significantly slow down your site.

- Use the Right File Format: JPEGs are great for photographs, while PNGs are better for images that require transparency. Avoid using BMPs or TIFFs, as they are not web-friendly.

- Compress Images: Use image compression tools like TinyPNG, JPEGmini, or Photoshop's "Save for Web" option to reduce file sizes without sacrificing quality. This can drastically reduce load times.

- Lazy Loading: Implement lazy loading, a technique where images load only when they're about to enter the user's view. This reduces the initial load time and improves the user experience.

3. Minimize HTTP Requests

EVERY ELEMENT ON YOUR web page—images, scripts, stylesheets—requires an HTTP request. The more requests, the slower your site.

- Combine Files: Combine multiple CSS files into one and do the same for JavaScript files. This reduces the number of requests and speeds up load times.

- Use CSS Sprites: CSS sprites allow you to combine multiple images into a single file. The browser then loads the single file and displays the correct image portion. This is especially useful for icons and buttons.

- Reduce Plugins: If you're using a platform like WordPress, minimize the number of plugins. Each plugin adds to the number of HTTP requests, so only use the ones that are essential.

4. Enable Browser Caching

BROWSER CACHING ALLOWS your site to store files on a visitor's device, so they don't have to be downloaded every time the user visits your site.

- Set Expiry Dates: By setting expiry dates on cached content, you can control how long files are stored on the user's device. Use tools like YSlow or Google PageSpeed Insights to identify which files should be cached.

- Leverage .htaccess: If you have access to your site's .htaccess file, you can manually enable caching and set expiry dates for different types of content.

5. Minify CSS, JavaScript, and HTML

MINIFICATION IS THE process of removing unnecessary characters (like spaces and line breaks) from your code, making it smaller and faster to load.

- Use Online Tools: Tools like UglifyJS for JavaScript, CSSNano for CSS, and HTMLMinifier for HTML can help you minify your files.

- Automate the Process: If you're using a build tool like Gulp or Webpack, you can automate minification during your site's build process, ensuring your files are always optimized.

6. Optimize Your Music Player

IF YOUR SITE FEATURES a music player, it's important to ensure it doesn't slow down your site.

- Use Streaming Services: Instead of hosting large audio files on your server, embed music from streaming platforms like SoundCloud,

Spotify, or Bandcamp. These platforms are optimized for fast loading and offer high-quality streaming.

- Optimize Embedded Players: If you're embedding a music player, make sure it loads asynchronously, meaning it won't hold up the rest of your site's content from loading.

7. Enable Gzip Compression

GZIP COMPRESSION REDUCES the size of your files before they are sent to the browser, which can significantly decrease loading times.

- Activate Gzip: Most web servers, including Apache and Nginx, support Gzip compression. You can enable it through your site's .htaccess file or via your server's configuration settings.

- Check Compression: Use online tools like Gtmetrix or Google PageSpeed Insights to check if Gzip compression is enabled on your site and see the difference in file sizes.

8. Use a Lightweight Theme

IF YOU'RE USING A CONTENT management system (CMS) like WordPress, the theme you choose can greatly impact your site's speed.

- Choose a Fast Theme: Opt for themes that are built with performance in mind. Avoid overly complex themes with excessive animations, sliders, and widgets that can slow down your site.

- Custom vs. Premade Themes: If you have the budget, consider a custom-built theme that's optimized for your specific needs. Otherwise, choose a well-coded, lightweight premade theme and customize it to suit your style.

9. Monitor Your Website's Performance

REGULARLY MONITORING your website's performance helps you identify issues and make necessary adjustments.

- Use Speed Testing Tools: Tools like Google PageSpeed Insights, Pingdom, and Gtmetrix provide detailed reports on your site's speed and offer suggestions for improvement.

- Analyze Traffic Spikes: If you experience slowdowns during traffic spikes, consider using a service like Cloudflare to manage the increased load or upgrading your hosting plan to handle more visitors.

10. Keep Your Site Updated

KEEPING YOUR SITE'S software up-to-date is crucial for both security and performance.

- Update CMS and Plugins: Regularly update your CMS, plugins, and themes to ensure they're optimized and free from vulnerabilities that could slow down your site.

- Remove Unused Plugins and Themes: Deactivate and delete any plugins or themes you're not using. Even inactive plugins can slow down your site, so keep your installation clean.

Conclusion

OPTIMIZING YOUR WEBSITE'S loading times is essential for keeping your audience engaged and improving your overall online presence. With the right strategies, you can ensure that your site is fast, efficient, and provides a great user experience, even if you're working with limited resources. By choosing the right hosting, optimizing your images, minimizing HTTP requests, and staying on top of updates, you can create a site that not only looks great but

also performs at its best. Remember, in the digital age, speed is not just a luxury—it's a necessity.

DIY Music Videos: Solving Lighting and Filming Challenges

Creating a music video is a powerful way to visually express your music and connect with your audience. However, if you're an independent artist, budget constraints can make producing a professional-looking video seem daunting. The good news is that you don't need expensive gear or a big crew to create a compelling music video. With some creativity and a few practical tips, you can solve common lighting and filming challenges to produce a video that looks polished and professional. Here's how.

1. Plan Your Video Concept Carefully

BEFORE DIVING INTO filming, it's essential to plan your video concept. A well-thought-out plan will help you make the most of your resources and avoid unnecessary expenses.

- Storyboarding: Sketch out your ideas in a storyboard. This doesn't have to be artistically perfect—just a simple outline of scenes and shots will do. Storyboarding helps you visualize the flow of the video and ensures you capture all the necessary footage.

- Location Scouting: Look for locations that align with your video's theme. Public spaces, parks, and even your home can serve as excellent settings. Consider the natural lighting available in these locations, as it can save you time and money on lighting setups.

- Keep It Simple: Don't overcomplicate your concept. A straightforward idea executed well can be far more impactful than an elaborate one that stretches your resources thin.

2. Use Natural Light to Your Advantage

LIGHTING IS ONE OF the most critical elements in video production. While professional lighting setups can be expensive, you can achieve great results by harnessing natural light.

- Golden Hour: The golden hour, shortly after sunrise or before sunset, provides soft, warm light that is flattering for video. Plan your shoot around these times to make the most of this natural lighting.

- Cloudy Days: Overcast days offer diffused, even lighting that eliminates harsh shadows. This is ideal for outdoor shoots, as it provides consistent lighting without the need for reflectors or additional equipment.

- Window Light: For indoor shoots, position your subject near a large window to take advantage of natural light. Use sheer curtains to diffuse the light if it's too harsh.

3. DIY Lighting Solutions

IF YOU NEED ADDITIONAL lighting, there are several budget-friendly options you can create yourself.

- Reflectors: A simple reflector can bounce light onto your subject, filling in shadows and creating a more even look. You can make your own reflector using a piece of white foam board or aluminum foil.

- Household Lamps: Standard lamps can serve as effective lighting tools. Use lampshades to diffuse the light, or bounce the light off walls or ceilings for a softer effect. Experiment with different bulbs to achieve the color temperature you want.

- LED Light Panels: Affordable LED light panels can provide consistent, adjustable light for your shoot. They're portable, easy to set up, and can be powered by batteries, making them perfect for on-the-go filming.

4. Stabilize Your Shots

SHAKY FOOTAGE CAN MAKE even the best-planned video look amateurish. Stabilizing your shots is essential for creating a professional-looking video.

- Tripod: Invest in a good tripod for steady, stable shots. There are many affordable options available that are lightweight and easy to use.

- DIY Stabilizers: If you don't have a tripod, try using a stack of books, a sturdy table, or even a pile of blankets to stabilize your camera.

- Handheld Techniques: If you're shooting handheld, use both hands to hold the camera, keep your elbows close to your body, and move smoothly. You can also use the camera's in-built stabilization features if available.

5. Use Your Smartphone Effectively

MODERN SMARTPHONES come equipped with powerful cameras that are more than capable of shooting high-quality video.

- Manual Settings: Explore your phone's camera settings and experiment with manual controls like ISO, shutter speed, and focus. This allows you to have more control over the final look of your video.

- External Lenses: Consider investing in external lenses designed for smartphones. These lenses can give you a wider field of view, a sharper image, or even macro capabilities, expanding your creative options.

- Filmic Apps: Use apps like Filmic Pro to gain more control over your phone's camera settings. These apps often include features like manual focus, exposure controls, and color grading tools.

6. Focus on Composition

GOOD COMPOSITION CAN elevate your video and make it look more professional, even if you're working with basic equipment.

- Rule of Thirds: Divide your frame into thirds, both horizontally and vertically, and place your subject along these lines or at their intersections. This creates a balanced and visually appealing shot.

- Leading Lines: Use natural lines in your environment, such as roads, fences, or pathways, to draw the viewer's eye towards your subject.

- Depth of Field: Create depth in your shots by including elements in the foreground, middle ground, and background. This adds a sense of dimension and makes your video more engaging.

7. Edit with Care

EDITING IS WHERE YOUR footage comes together to create the final product. Even if you're editing on a budget, you can achieve professional results with careful attention to detail.

- Free Editing Software: Programs like DaVinci Resolve, HitFilm Express, and iMovie offer powerful editing tools at no cost. These tools provide a range of features for cutting, color grading, and adding effects to your video.

- Color Grading: Color grading can significantly enhance the look of your video. Use it to correct any lighting inconsistencies and to create a cohesive visual style.

- Keep It Simple: Don't overdo it with transitions and effects. Simple cuts and subtle transitions are often more effective than flashy effects that can distract from the music and visuals.

8. Test and Adjust

BEFORE THE ACTUAL SHOOT, it's a good idea to do a test run. This allows you to troubleshoot any issues and make adjustments before you start filming.

- Lighting Test: Set up your lighting and film a short test clip. Review the footage to ensure the lighting is consistent and flattering.

- Sound Check: If your video includes live sound or dialogue, do a sound check to ensure clarity and minimize background noise. Consider using an external microphone for better audio quality.

- Rehearsal: Run through your scenes or performance to get comfortable with the camera and the space. This will make the actual shoot smoother and more efficient.

Conclusion

CREATING A PROFESSIONAL-looking music video on a budget is entirely possible with the right approach and a bit of creativity. By planning carefully, making the most of natural light, using DIY lighting solutions, and paying attention to composition and editing, you can overcome common filming challenges and produce a video that truly represents your music. Remember, the key to a great music video is not how much money you spend, but how effectively you use the resources you have. With these tips in hand, you're well on your way to creating a visually compelling and polished music video, even on a shoestring budget.

Navigating Copyright: How to Protect Your Original Music

As a musician, your creations are your most valuable assets. Whether you're writing lyrics, composing melodies, or producing tracks, your music represents countless hours of hard work and creativity. That's why understanding copyright and knowing how to protect your original music is crucial. In this blog post, we'll cover the basics of copyright, explain how it works, and provide steps to safeguard your musical creations.

What is Copyright?

COPYRIGHT IS A LEGAL protection granted to the creators of original works, including music, literature, art, and more. It gives the creator exclusive rights to use, distribute, and profit from their work. For musicians, this means that as soon as you create an original piece of music, you automatically own the copyright to it.

Key Rights Under Copyright Law

When you own the copyright to your music, you have several important rights:

- Reproduction Rights: You have the exclusive right to make copies of your music.

- Distribution Rights: You control how your music is distributed, whether through physical copies or digital downloads.

- Public Performance Rights: You have the right to control public performances of your music, including concerts, radio broadcasts, and streaming.

- Derivative Works: You can create new works based on your original music, such as remixes or adaptations.

- Synchronization Rights: You control how your music is used in combination with visual media, like films, TV shows, or advertisements.

Steps to Safeguard Your Music

While copyright protection is automatic, there are several steps you can take to strengthen your legal position and ensure your rights are fully protected.

1. Document Your Work

KEEPING DETAILED RECORDS of your creative process is a simple yet effective way to prove ownership of your music.

- Keep Drafts: Save all drafts, recordings, and notes related to your compositions. These can serve as evidence of the evolution of your work.

- Timestamp Your Files: Ensure that all digital files are timestamped. This can help establish a timeline of creation, which is useful in the event of a dispute.

- Consider a Copyright Notice: While not required, adding a copyright notice to your work can serve as a public declaration of your ownership. It typically includes the © symbol, your name, and the year of creation.

2. Register Your Copyright

WHILE COPYRIGHT IS automatic, registering your music with the relevant authorities provides additional legal protection and benefits.

- Why Register? Registration allows you to take legal action against anyone who infringes on your copyright. It also makes it easier to prove ownership in court.

- How to Register in the U.S.: In the United States, you can register your music with the U.S. Copyright Office. This can be done online by submitting a form, a copy of your work, and a small fee.

- International Registration: If you're outside the U.S., check your country's specific copyright registration process. Many countries are part of international treaties that recognize copyright across borders.

3. Use Digital Rights Management (DRM)

DIGITAL RIGHTS MANAGEMENT (DRM) tools can help you control how your music is used and distributed online.

- Watermarking: Embed a digital watermark in your music files. This invisible mark can trace the origin of your work and deter unauthorized copying.

- DRM Software: Use DRM software to restrict how your music files are used, preventing unauthorized copying, sharing, or distribution.

- Licensing Platforms: Consider distributing your music through platforms that offer DRM protections, like iTunes, Spotify, or Bandcamp.

4. Consider Publishing and Licensing Agreements

IF YOU PLAN TO MONETIZE your music, understanding publishing and licensing is crucial.

- Music Publishing: A music publisher can help manage your rights, collect royalties, and secure placements for your music in media. They typically take a percentage of your earnings in exchange for their services.

- Licensing Agreements: If someone wants to use your music, such as in a commercial or film, you'll need a licensing agreement. This legally outlines how your music will be used, the duration, and the compensation.

5. Monitor Your Work

KEEPING AN EYE ON HOW your music is being used can help you catch unauthorized uses and protect your rights.

- Use Monitoring Services: There are services that monitor radio, TV, and digital platforms for unauthorized use of your music. Companies like ASCAP, BMI, and SoundExchange offer such services.

- Search Online: Regularly search for your music online to ensure it's not being distributed without your permission. Tools like Google Alerts can notify you if your music appears on new websites.

- Take Action if Necessary: If you find that someone is using your music without permission, you have the right to take action. This can range from sending a cease-and-desist letter to pursuing legal action for copyright infringement.

6. Understand Fair Use and Public Domain

NOT ALL USES OF YOUR music require permission. Understanding the concepts of fair use and public domain can help you navigate these exceptions.

- Fair Use: Certain uses of your music may be considered fair use, such as for commentary, criticism, or parody. However, this is a complex area of law, and what qualifies as fair use is often determined on a case-by-case basis.

- Public Domain: After a certain period, works enter the public domain, meaning they are no longer protected by copyright and can be used freely. However, this period can vary by country and work type, so it's important to understand the specific rules that apply to your music.

Conclusion

PROTECTING YOUR ORIGINAL music is essential to ensuring that you maintain control over your creative work and receive the recognition and compensation you deserve. By understanding the basics of copyright and taking proactive steps to safeguard your music, you can protect your rights and navigate the music industry with confidence. Remember, your music is your intellectual property—take the necessary steps to protect it.

A Beginner's Guide to Becoming a Music Producer

Starting Your Journey To Becoming A Music Producer

Introduction

SO, YOU'RE THINKING about diving into the world of music production? Awesome! Whether you're dreaming of crafting the next big hit or just looking to explore your musical talents, starting your journey as a music producer can be an exhilarating experience. Let's break down what you need to know and how you can get started on this exciting path.

This article provides a comprehensive guide to becoming a music producer, covering topics such as the basics of music production, the different types of music producers, and tips for success.

Understanding Music Production

WHAT IS MUSIC PRODUCTION?

Music production involves the creation and manipulation of sound to produce music. This includes everything from recording and mixing to mastering and finalizing tracks. Essentially, it's about taking raw audio and shaping it into a polished, cohesive piece of art.

The Role of a Music Producer

A music producer wears many hats. They're not just responsible for the technical aspects of recording; they also help guide the creative process. This can involve arranging music, suggesting changes, and even working directly with artists to bring their vision to life.

Key Skills Required

To be a successful music producer, you'll need a mix of technical skills and creativity. Understanding sound engineering, mastering software, and having a good ear for music are crucial. But don't forget, communication and collaboration skills are equally important.

Setting Up Your Home Studio

CHOOSING THE RIGHT Equipment

Computer and Software

Your computer is the heart of your home studio. You'll need a reliable machine capable of handling music production software. Speaking of which, selecting the right DAW (Digital Audio Workstation) is essential. Popular DAWs include Ableton Live, FL Studio, and Logic Pro.

Audio Interface

An audio interface is crucial for recording high-quality audio. It acts as a bridge between your instruments and your computer, converting analog signals into digital ones.

Monitors and Headphones

Good studio monitors and headphones are essential for accurate sound representation. Investing in high-quality monitors will ensure that your mixes translate well across different playback systems.

Acoustic Treatment for Your Space

Even the best equipment won't be effective if your room isn't acoustically treated. Proper treatment helps reduce sound reflections and enhances the accuracy of your mixes. This can involve adding bass traps, diffusers, and acoustic panels.

Learning the Basics

MUSIC THEORY FUNDAMENTALS

Understanding basic music theory is crucial for any music producer. It helps you structure your compositions, create harmonies, and understand the relationship between different musical elements.

Understanding DAWs (Digital Audio Workstations)

DAWs are the software platforms where you'll do most of your work. Familiarize yourself with the features and capabilities of your chosen DAW, including recording, editing, and mixing functions.

Basic Recording Techniques

Learn the basics of recording techniques, such as microphone placement, gain staging, and track layering. These fundamentals will help you capture high-quality audio for your projects.

Developing Your Unique Sound

FINDING YOUR STYLE

As you begin producing, you'll start to develop your unique sound. Experiment with different genres and styles to discover what resonates with you.

Experimenting with Genres

Don't be afraid to step out of your comfort zone. Exploring various genres can broaden your skill set and inspire creativity.

Building a Signature Sound

Over time, aim to develop a signature sound that sets you apart from other producers. This could be a particular style, technique, or a blend of genres.

Networking and Collaboration

CONNECTING WITH OTHER Musicians

Networking is vital in the music industry. Connect with other musicians, producers, and industry professionals to expand your opportunities and gain new insights.

Collaborating on Projects

Collaboration can lead to exciting new directions in your music. Working with others can also help you learn and grow as a producer.

Using Social Media to Your Advantage

Social media platforms are powerful tools for promoting your work. Share your projects, connect with fans, and engage with the music community online.

Marketing Yourself as a Music Producer

CREATING AN ONLINE Presence

Build a professional website and social media profiles to showcase your work. An online presence can help you attract clients and fans.

Building a Portfolio

Your portfolio should highlight your best work. Include samples of your music, testimonials, and any notable collaborations or projects.

Utilizing Platforms for Exposure

Consider using platforms like SoundCloud, YouTube, and Bandcamp to distribute your music and reach a wider audience.

Challenges and How to Overcome Them

COMMON OBSTACLES

Every producer faces challenges, from creative blocks to technical issues. Identifying common obstacles can help you prepare and find solutions.

Staying Motivated

Maintaining motivation is crucial. Set goals, track your progress, and celebrate your achievements to stay inspired.

Continuous Learning and Improvement

The music industry is always evolving. Keep learning new techniques, exploring new software, and staying updated on trends to continuously improve your skills.

Staying Inspired

FINDING INSPIRATION

Inspiration can come from anywhere – other music, nature, or even everyday life. Stay open to new experiences and ideas.

Overcoming Creative Blocks

Creative blocks are a natural part of the process. Try changing your routine, exploring different genres, or collaborating with others to overcome them.

Keeping Up with Trends

Stay informed about industry trends and emerging technologies. This can help you stay relevant and incorporate new ideas into your music.

Conclusion

Starting your journey as a music producer is both challenging and rewarding. By understanding the basics, setting up your studio, developing your sound, and continuously learning, you can carve out your place in the music industry. Embrace the journey, stay passionate, and keep pushing the boundaries of your creativity.

FAQs

WHAT EQUIPMENT DO I need to start as a music producer?

To get started, you'll need a computer with a DAW, an audio interface, studio monitors or headphones, and a good microphone. Basic acoustic treatment can also improve your recording environment.

How do I choose the right DAW for me?

Consider your workflow preferences and budget. Try out different DAWs through trial versions to see which one feels most intuitive and meets your needs.

How important is networking in the music industry?

Networking is crucial. It helps you connect with other professionals, collaborate on projects, and find new opportunities.

What are some common mistakes new producers make?

Common mistakes include neglecting acoustic treatment, overlooking basic music theory, and not investing in quality equipment. Avoiding these can help you produce better music.

How can I keep my music production skills sharp?

Keep learning and experimenting. Take courses, read industry blogs, and practice regularly to refine your skills and stay updated with new trends.

Also by Neil J Milliner

Milton Keynes UK
Ingram Content Group UK Ltd.
UKHW042003281024
450365UK00003B/139